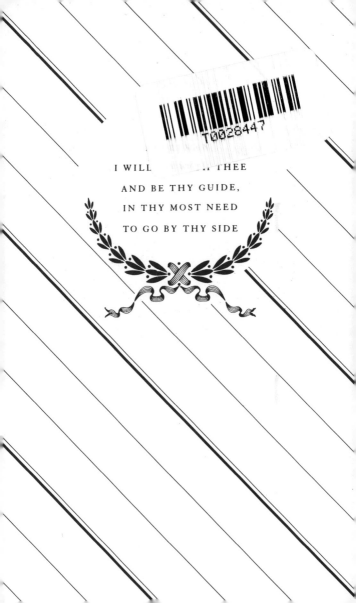

I WILL [...] THEE
AND BE THY GUIDE,
IN THY MOST NEED
TO GO BY THY SIDE

EVERYMAN'S LIBRARY
POCKET POETS

RUMI

UNSEEN POEMS

••••••••••••••••••••

TRANSLATED AND
EDITED BY
BRAD GOOCH AND
MARYAM MORTAZ

EVERYMAN'S LIBRARY
POCKET POETS

Alfred A. Knopf New York London Toronto

THIS IS A BORZOI BOOK
PUBLISHED BY ALFRED A. KNOPF

This edition first published in Everyman's Library, 2019
Translation copyright © 2019 by Brad Gooch and Maryam Mortaz

Third printing (US)

The translation of Rumi's "Where did the handsome beloved go?"
was originally published in *Poetry* Magazine, November 2017,
Volume CCXI, Number 2.

www.randomhouse/everymans
www.everymanslibrary.co.uk

ISBN 978-1-101-90810-5 (US)
978-1-84159-816-1 (UK)

A CIP catalogue reference for this book is available from the British Library

Library of Congress Cataloging-in-Publication Data
Names: Jalåal al-Dåin Råumåi, Maulana, 1207–1273, author. | Gooch, Brad, 1952–
translator. | Mortaz, Maryam, translator.
Title: Rumi: unseen poems / translated and edited by Brad Gooch and
Maryam Mortaz.
Description: New York: Alfred A. Knopf, 2019. | Series: Everyman's library
pocket poets
Identifiers: LCCN 2019013642 (print) | LCCN 2019017237 (ebook) |
ISBN 9781101908112 (ebook) | ISBN 9781101908105 (hardcover: alk. paper)
Subjects: LCSH: Jalåal al-Dåin Råumåi, Maulana, 1207–1273—Translations
into English.
Classification: LCC PK6480.E5 (ebook) | LCC PK6480.E5 G66 2019 (print) |
DDC 891/.5511—dc23
LC record available at https://lccn.loc.gov/2019013642

Typography by Peter B. Willberg
Typeset in the UK by Input Data Services Ltd, Isle Abbotts, Somerset
Printed and bound in Germany by GGP Media GmbH, Pössneck

Contents

5

Foreword

"Love speaks a hundred different languages," exulted Rumi. He might well have said the same of his own ardently recited and ecstatically translated poems of love, which have found their way around the world like "a hundred thousand flames" – to use a favorite Rumi image – since his death in the Turkish city of Konya in 1321. A Persian-speaking poet, displaced from Central Asia during the Mongol terrors and winding up with his family in the Seljuk Empire in Asia Minor, after years of traveling through such thriving Muslim cities as Baghdad, Damascus, and Aleppo, Rumi expressed a polyglot civilization in poetry that segues easily among Persian, Arabic (especially the Arabic of the *Quran*), Turkish, and Greek. Over seven centuries he has been translated into dozens of languages and claimed as a "national" poet by Afghans, Iranians, and Turks alike.

The heartbeats of American and English poets and translators have often quickened to Rumi as well, beginning with Ralph Waldo Emerson, who translated an exquisitely mystical poem from the German of Rückert: "Of Paradise am I the Peacock, / Who has escaped from his nest." The Cambridge University professor R. A. Nicholson devoted his life to translating Rumi's six-volume spiritual epic, *The Masnavi*, often while dressed in Sufi robes and a tall round hat. At a poetry workshop in the United States in the 1970s, Robert Bly presented

11

the young poet Coleman Barks with a volume of the decidedly literal translations of another Cambridge scholar, A. J. Arberry. "These poems need to be released from their cages," said Bly, and the ensuing flutter of free-verse – almost beat – renditions led to Rumi's status as the "best-selling poet in America."

Yet in the decade since I started seeking writings left behind by Rumi, as I researched my biography of his life and times, *Rumi's Secret*, I discovered that wide swathes of the poetry were still lying dormant, mostly unseen and unheard by the English reading public. Crucial to this realization has been my collaborator in the translations in this collection, Maryam Mortaz. An Iranian poet and writer living in New York City, Maryam began as my tutor in her native tongue – Persian, or *Farsi* – even helping long-distance when I studied in Persian immersion programs at University of Texas at Austin and University of Wisconsin at Madison. As the book expanded so did Maryam's role, and we jointly translated all the prose and poetry in the biography. When we were stumped by swerves in Rumi's thought, she would call her friend Qhasem Hasheminejad, a poet, novelist, and scholar in Iran; when I was in Tehran, he visited me in my hotel lobby and fixed me with his wise gaze while edgily wearing a Sufi skullcap in public. (The mystical practices of Sufism are discouraged by conservative and religious leaders, as they were in Rumi's day.)

Rumi's *Masnavi* has been thoroughly translated into

English, first by Nicholson in England and now in an ongoing project by Jawid Mojaddedi at Rutgers. Indeed, many current translations of Rumi's poetry are excerpts from this epic, with titles added. (Rumi never titled any of his poems.) Yet there remain the lyric ghazals, similar to sonnets in length and impact, often with *radif*, or repeating phrases punctuating line ends. Dizzyingly creative, Rumi wrote more than 3,000 ghazals; of these, only about half have been translated into English directly from Persian. He also wrote about 2,000 robaiyat, the pithy quatrain form made famous in Edward Fitzgerald's Victorian renditions of Omar Khayyam – an earlier poet whose chill blasts of skepticism likely did not move Rumi. A scholarly translation of all of Rumi's robaiyat exists, but those in popular circulation number only about 400, leaving the majority of these short haiku-like poems underappreciated.

An obvious question is why so many poems by a celebrated poet have been overlooked. In part it's an accident of history. Much translation in the past half-century has consisted of standing on the shoulders of Nicholson or Arberry, whose cumulative two-volume edition included about 500 ghazals. Poets have sprung these cages either by infusing them with more spirit or tracing back to the originals in Persian and producing new versions. Yet Arberry, a formidable scholar of Arabic, Persian, and Islamic studies, had his own preferences. We feel he left out some of the *poet's poet* works of lilting beauty –

13

lacking any special messages of wisdom – that gave us pleasure. At the other extreme, many popular recent translations avoid references to Islam or allusions to Persian literature and culture that were perhaps judged too foreign or off-putting. I've met fans of Rumi – who had his poems read at their wedding – who were surprised to find out he was not a Buddhist.

A number of the poems in the quarry we mined have been understandably bypassed over the years: Rumi repeats himself, and some of his uses of the stock imagery of Persian poetry – stars and moons, nightingales and roses – are fresher than others. A few are impossibly mind-bending as Rumi leads us on travels into the ineffable with only broken language and twisting syntax as our guide. (He broke the rules more than any other classical Persian poet.) We tried to include as many of these puzzles as could be solved, as well as a few favorite poems previously translated by others that we could not resist including. We were transported when we found some of our repeating lines faintly evoking the music of the originals or, most certainly, when we came across gleaming works that were as beautiful or philosophically compelling as anything we had ever read of Rumi's. Our intention was to find a middle way between academic loyalty and wildly inventive freedom, a medium that might articulate both the personal poems of aching human love, to Rumi's beloved companion and teacher, Shams of Tabriz, and those of divine love, in his hymns to God that soar like Mohammad's winged horse Buraq.

Rumi cast himself as a reluctant poet. His attitude was a bit like that of Marianne Moore in her poem "Poetry," which begins, "I, too, dislike it." Yet his motives were different. Rumi was a religious leader, composing verses as he whirled himself into trances to annihilate ordinary reality and language in a mystical union with love itself. This urgent and sincere spirit is perhaps responsible for the way the voice of this medieval poet shines through all manner of translations, making him, as a publisher once said to me, "translation-proof." Persian poets often put their signature; or *takhallos*, like a tag in last lines. Rumi occasionally used "Silence" as his tag. For him, the most successful poems were failures, breaking apart in silence. "Rip this poem apart like an old piece of cloth," he wrote, "To set meaning free from words, wind, and air." We hope this collection will provide fresh glimpses into Rumi's sublime "world of silence ... like a bird's wing."

BRAD GOOCH

Where is the grace I saw in your face all night?

Where is the grace I saw in your face all night?
Such a sweet story I heard from you, all night.

Although your flame burned the moth of my heart,
I circled the flame of your beautiful face, all night.

Before your beautiful moonlike face, night veiled itself.
I ripped apart the veil of night, all night.

My soul, full of joy, licked itself like a cat.
Like a baby, I sucked my thumb, all night.

My chest, like a beehive, full of buzzing,
From you, the source of honey, I drank nectar,
    all night.

The trap of night was set, capturing everyone's souls.
My heart, like a bird, throbbed in that trap, all night.

All souls, like doves, are under his command.
Within its trap, I desired him, all night.

All flowers seek refuge in this meadow

All flowers seek refuge in this meadow,
Where autumn never comes and roses never die.

A tree full of green branches grows in the middle of
    the desert.
Whoever sleeps in its shadow will wake up delirious.

That sky is like the heavens, souls yearn to travel
    there,
Where Saturn lacks the courage to challenge Venus.

You are a delicate pearl, found in no quarry or mine,
With the slightest hint from your heart, you shed
    a tear.

**Today the line between a stranger and me,
I do not know**

Today the line between a stranger and me,
   I do not know.
So drunk that the road to my own house,
   I do not know.

In love with you, I freed myself from sensible intellect.
Anything but the desperation of a madman,
   I do not know.

In the garden, I see nothing but a vision of my friend's
      face.
Anything but the branches swaying in drunken ecstasy,
   I do not know.

He said, "In this trap, somebody placed bait."
I'm swooning and in this trap even the bait,
   I do not know.

Today don't read this fable and its charming words.
Spells won't work. Of heart and fable, I do not know.

Like a comb, my heart tangled in your curly hair,
In ecstasy, the line between comb and hair,
   I do not know.

Pour the wine but don't ask how many cups I've drunk.
Thinking of you, the line between wine and cup,
   I do not know.

I lost myself but am longing to lose myself more

I lost myself but am longing to lose myself more.
I tell your eyes that I am longing to be as drunk as you.

I don't long for a crown. I don't long for a throne.
I long to bow to the ground in your service.

My beautiful beloved grabs me by the throat.
You say, "What do you long for?" I say, "This!"

I long for the morning breezes to breathe.
I have my breath but long for someone to tell
    secrets to.

I am in the circle of pilgrims. I am safe from
    misfortune.
I am wax beneath your seal, longing for the press of
    your ring.

Another moon is hiding inside the moon.
I am sure of this truth as I look into your true eyes.

No interpreter for my fire

No interpreter for my fire.
No language for the secrets of my heart.

No sighs to express my pain.
No souls to share my sighs.

No pearl rising from the sea.
No calm sea, not even for a moment.

No words giving birth to meaning.
No words clearly spoken.

Language is a stream of meaning.
How can the sea ever pass through a stream?

In the world of souls, every soul is a world.
No word can ever contain the world.

When your love inflamed my heart

When your love inflamed my heart,
All I had was burned to ashes except your love.
I put logic and learning and books on the shelf,
And learned the art of poetry and song.

**Out of love for you, every strand of my hair
turned into lines of poetry**

Out of love for you, every strand of my hair turned into
   lines of poetry.
Out of delight in you, every part of my body turned
   into honey.

The sun filled with your beauty, the sea with your
   honey,
Every atom of the sun turned into a master of all
   skills.

Out of desire for you, my heart took flight.
Seeing your face, my soul turned into a cluster of stars.

Rise up, rise up, I'm an ocean of poetry

Rise up, rise up, I'm an ocean of poetry.
Other than love, other than love, I have nothing to do.

In this land, in this land, in this empty field,
Other than mercy, other than love, I don't plant any
    seeds.

I'm so drunk. I'm so drunk, from my friend the king.
Come close, come close, I'm spreading wide my arms.

What do I know? What do I know? What I drank last
    night!
Today, the whole day, I'm tired and hung over.

Don't ask, don't ask, about the state of truth.
Since I worship the wine, I'm not counting the cups.

You are not drunk. You have not drunk the wine.
What do you know, what do you know, of what I hunt?

I don't fall backwards on the land. I'm no cheap straw
    mat.
I rise to the heavens. I'm a man of the highest heights.

Come back! Out of love for you, I turned into a madman

Come back! Out of love for you, I turned into a
    madman.
If I were a city, I would have turned into a ruin.

Out of love for you, cut off from home and family,
I turned into a companion of the pain of your love.

I was so listless. I could no longer speak.
When I saw your face, I turned into a man of courage.

When I saw your soul inside my soul,
I turned into a stranger with everyone I knew.

Night and day, I was reading stories of lovers.
Now, out of love for you, I have turned into a fable
    of love.

Sing with love, of the pain of loss, speak

Sing with love, of the pain of loss, speak.
Either in Persian or in Latin, speak.

Whether Roman or Arab, I only want you.
Of your beauty, purity, and mercy, speak.

You burn down and you build up. You illuminate the
    world.
If you are the sun or the moon, fire or wax, speak.

If someone says, "The fire is cold," don't believe him.
Smoke and incense, eternal and everlasting, speak.

My flying heart, trying to escape this ruin of a body,
If you are a falcon, fly aloft. If you are an owl, speak.

My heart is a pen held in the beloved's hand

My heart is a pen held in the beloved's hand,
Writing this way tonight and that way tomorrow.

He shaves his reed pen for writing notes and books and
    more.
The pen says: "I surrender. You know who I am,
    O Lord."

Sometimes his face black from ink, sometimes rubbing
    it in his hair,
Sometimes holding the pen upside down, sometimes
    using it for work.

Scraping the pen across a single sheet of the world, he
    cuts off its head.
On another sheet, he saves two planets from a terrible
    collision.

The glory and splendor of the pen matches the dignity
    of the scribe,
Whether in the hand of a king or in the hand of a
    general.

He splits the tip to find what it knows.
The physician knows what is best for the patient.

The pen is unable to offer praise in its own words.
The pen is unable to refuse to sign its own assent.

Whether I call it a pen or I call it a pennant,
It is both aware and unaware, such unaware awareness!

The mind cannot fully explain such contraries,
A kind of artful artlessness, a marvelous form freely
    formed.

Oh voice of the rabab, where do you come from?

Oh voice of the rabab, where do you come from?
Full of fire, full of desire, and full of strife.
You are a spy from the heart, a message from
    the desert,
Your every cry reveals the secrets of the heart.

Your speech made me silent

Your speech made me silent.
Your delicious actions made me still.
When I escaped from your trap into the house of
    my heart,
My heart turned into a trap, and made me your
    prisoner.

Each moment a vision of him stirs my heart

Each moment a vision of him stirs my heart,
A new sunrise of goodwill and beauty.

O God, is this perfume of joy from paradise?
Or is it carried on the breeze of our reunion?

Is love dazzling my mind with his music?
Or is it drinking from the cup of his pure wine?

Or is it like a hawk that flies with love?
Or a flight of young doves taking wing?

He pokes his head through, from the unseen world,
Bringing me relief and delight with all his ecstasy.

Once again my heart is catching fire

Once again my heart is catching fire.
Leave it alone until it begins to blaze.

Burn, heart. In this lightning, be still.
A cloud of passion is covering my mind.

Once more my heart is dreaming.
Like a carpet, my heart's blood covers the ground.

Like a shadow, I disappear into oblivion,
As the great commander, the sun, invades the world.

Each night my heart, like a thief and traitor,
Steals the royal rubies from the king.

Where can he hide? Both thief and treasure?
Smuggling those weighty jewels beneath his arm?

My soul strives to flee from my body,
Yet my companion keeps pulling its feet to his chest.

Joyful to be wounded by his arrow, my heart
Grabs the bands of his turban in his teeth, not
    letting go.

My face is a hundred times brighter when I see your face

My face is a hundred times brighter when I see
    your face.
My soul is a hundred times happier when your soul
    is near.

When the mirror of my life is polished by your love,
The mirror of the world is no longer dull and dark.

The bird of my heart was beating and restless,
Until finding a nest in tranquility.

Without your eyes, my eyes have no mirror.
Without your day, my skylight has no light.

When I first saw you, my eyes said, "You are my light."
When I first found you, my soul said, "You are
    my soul."

Patience waited for you, gratitude gave thanks for you,
Poverty was ennobled by you, and filled with wealth.

Sometimes I come to your door, pounding on
    the wood.
Sometimes you come to my chest, knocking on
    my heart.

Morning breeze, take these messages to love,
So through your kind efforts, I may grow in purity.

Like a pen, my duty is to be at your service,
Like sugar cane, your duty is to make things sweet.

O Heart, find safety within me. If you separate
    from me,
You will disappear. If you don't, I will know that we
    are one.

A sweet seed said to the stone: "If I break,
I have an almond within. But you, what if you break?"

One night, wishing to say hello, I knocked on the door of the heart

One night, wishing to say hello, I knocked on the door
of the heart.
A voice called out, "Who's there?" I answered, "It's me,
the servant of the heart."

The shining light of the moon, through the half-
opened door,
Struck the hearts and eyes of passersby as I uttered the
beautiful name of the heart.

A wave of light from the heart's face filled the alley.
A jar of sunlight and moonlight waited to fill the cup of
the heart.

Knowledge wishes to lead but is always at the heart's
service.
The neck of knowledge is trapped within the noose
of the heart.

Cries have reached the heavens. The world is full of
turmoil.
The crowd has broken their chains, listening to the
message of the heart.

The heart's light has suffused the throne of the
    Almighty.
The soul is seated at the door gazing toward the roof of
    the heart.

"A dervish is no mere mortal," he only said this much
    to me,
The rest was just a glimpse into the silent words of
    the heart.

The whole world drunk with heart, helpless in the
    palm of the heart.
Surely the nine heavens are within the two steps of the
    traveling heart.

The beloved shines like the sun

The beloved shines like the sun,
And the lover, like an atom, whirls about him.
When the springtime breezes of love stir,
Each branch that is not dry begins to dance.

Who says the eternal one is dead?

Who says the eternal one is dead?
Who says the sun of hope is dead?
An enemy of the sun climbed on the roof,
Closed his eyes, and said, "The sun is dead!"

O Sunshine, fill the house once again with light

O Sunshine, fill the house once again with light.
Make my friends happy and my enemies blind.

Rise above the mountains. Turn stones into rubies.
With your heat, make sour grapes sweet again.

Sunshine, once again make the gardens green.
Fill fields and meadows with festivals and angels.

Physician of lovers and lantern of the sky,
Hold the hands of lovers and find a cure for the
    afflicted.

Don't hide the moon of your face behind clouds.
For a little while move this cloud far from that beauty.

If you want a world of darkness, keep your face hidden.
If you want a world full of light, reveal to us your face.

Since I am a servant of the sun, I speak of the sun

Since I am a servant of the sun, I speak of the sun.
I am not a worshiper of the night. I do not speak
    of dreams.

I am the messenger of the sun, the interpreter of
    the sun.
After I question him in secret, I will tell you his
    answers.

As tall as the sun, I shine my light into ruins.
Escaping from the castle, my speech is broken.

Higher than the treetops, I am far from the dirt.
Wrapped in layers, I speak only of the essence.

Although a fallen apple, I drop from a high tree.
Although drunk and intoxicated, I speak of virtue.

When my heart catches his scent in his dusty alley,
I am too humble to think of pouring water on his dust.

Pull the veil from your face, as your face is beautiful.
I am not allowed to speak when your face is veiled.

When your heart is hard as stone, I am iron melted
    by fire.
When you turn to delicate glass, I speak of cups
    of wine.

For the saffron of your face, I speak of the splendor
of tulips.
For the tears from the spouts of your eyes, I speak of
the clouds.

Since the sun gave birth to me, I swear to God I am
king.
I will not rise at night nor will I speak of moonlight.

If my enemy thinks I am praying to God out of fear,
I complain loudly and bemoan my pain and anguish.

How could I praise Abu Bakr in the company of Shia?
How could I praise the sorrow of Ali in the company
of Sunni?

When the rabab mourns, I throw myself across him
like a bow.
When the preacher delivers a sermon, I expound
eloquently.

I silence my tongue since my heart is burning.
Your heart would burn, too, if I spoke of my burning
heart.

Sun, riding atop the sky

Sun, riding atop the sky,
Cleverly turning yourself into a star,

Sometimes like a heart in the chest,
Sometimes sitting off to the side,

Sometimes standing far, far away,
Like a stranger looking on,

Sometimes a cure burning away sorrow,
Sometimes asking, "What is the cure for this sorrow?"

You tear me apart and sew me together.
The heart is better in pieces, in pieces.

Sometimes my heart cries like a baby.
You say to me, "Rock the cradle."

Sometimes you hold me like a nurse.
Sometimes you mount me like a rider,

Sometimes you appear with white hair, sometimes
    gray,
Sometimes as a child and sometimes an infant.

Am I spent? Or did you grab my tongue?
Quickly and strongly and cleverly!

I learned about love from your perfection

I learned about love from your perfection.
I learned about poetry and song from your beauty.
Through the curtain of my heart, I saw you dancing.
I learned how to dance from thinking about you.

You were silent and I made you a storyteller

You were silent and I made you a storyteller.
You were pious and I made you a singer.
In the world, you had no name or title.
I made you sit and tell of signs and symbols.

Being lost in being lost is my faith

Being lost in being lost is my faith.
Not existing in existence is my way of life.

When walking in the alley of my friend,
I am riding the white horse of paradise,

Instantly passing through a hundred worlds,
Feeling as if I am taking a single step.

Why keep circling the world? My friend
Is in the midst of my sweet soul.

Shams of Tabriz, the pride of saints,
The "S" of his name is my "Salvation."

Lovers carry another world within

Lovers carry another world within,
But my love for my beloved gives another joy.

Enlightened hearts know things unseen,
But my beloved's heart has another seer.

Full of joy, wisdom's tongue turns into an ear
    for secrets,
But my beloved's secret has another translator.

By his grace, the eyes of the soul see a silver land,
But as you know, my beloved's moon has another sky.

Wisdom, love, and knowledge are ladders to the truth,
But my beloved's truth has another ladder.

At night, the king of intellect and his watchman travel
    far away,
But my beloved's soul goes far away with another
    watchman.

Lovers grow heartsick on the path of intellect,
But a voice from above says, "The heart has another
    heartland."

You keep complaining about a stolen heart.
Close your mouth! My lover speaks another language.

Shams of Tabriz is a candle, surrounded by moths.
Within the eyes of the heart, he has another eye.

Last night I was aching with love for Shams al-Din

Last night I was aching with love for Shams al-Din,
Lifting my soul towards the highest heaven.

Separated from his face, the lover of my soul,
I only have need for his love alone.

I am forever polishing the body of my soul,
As an offering for his love that lifts my soul.

Even if his love offered me a hundred different souls,
I would still be polishing myself in this marketplace.

Like a harp, I am lost in ecstasy,
Playing the scale of the music of lovers.

Within that music, one scale exists.
In the rays of its light, I see all other scales.

At every moment towards the music of love,
I make my way, more artfully, more artfully.

Through the stars, through the strings of the harp,
The moon, shining in all its fullness,

The rising sun shows his face from Tabriz,
Drawing my heart from the cloak of myself.

The rays of his sunlight are spreading farther

The rays of his sunlight are spreading farther,
With delight and delirium, love and simplicity.

Illuminated by you, the world shrinks. Who are you?
Are you the talisman of the heart or the treasure
    of souls?

A most excellent pen drew all the features of your face,
A pen that was able to divine messages not yet written.

You take away life from the six directions of the world.
Where the world used to be, you now plant love.

O heart, since the royal falcon hunted you,
You are able to translate the secret language of birds.

Such translations! You are now a towering Simorgh.
With the eyes of the soul you can see beyond a hundred
    Solomons.

Seeking you, my shoes of faith and doubt were torn
    apart.
You are a thousand years beyond faith and doubt.

When you rise at dawn, the soul's cock crows,
"Come, like the soul and the world; leave like a king."

My spirit has been nurtured by Shams of Tabriz.
From the garden of spirits, I have plucked for him a
    basil plant.

You found the hidden king, he wrote

You found the hidden king, he wrote.
You tasted the wine of heaven, he wrote.

The beloved of Khotan, the living meadows,
You dragged into the rose garden, he wrote.

O soul of the sweetheart, O essence of sugar,
You are the moon, the king, the festival, he wrote.

A message from the drunken ones, the wanderers,
For the lock of joy there is a key, he wrote.

So handsome and tall, such sweet medicine,
You stir the wine in your head, he wrote.

My heart, happily you wept for Shams of Tabriz,
You chose the chosen one, he wrote.

The beloved came to comfort and console me, secretly

The beloved came to comfort and console me, secretly.
The flirtatious king came at night like a shining moon,
    secretly.

He put his hand on my mouth, meaning be silent.
His eyes were saying to me, let us begin, secretly.

Drunk on his kindness, I broke the rose garden's gate
And began stealing roses from the garden, secretly.

I told him, "My beloved, you are so clever and crafty,
Conjure a powerful spell, you clever one, secretly.

Put your lips on my ear since it's night and we're alone.
Wait until a wind rustles through our secrets, secretly.

Moon, don't kill the mysteries of lovers! Be silent!
Play the strings of the harp of desire, secretly.

Smiling beloved, give me a secret gift,
Those two rubies, sweet and soulful, secretly.

All the drunken gossips are passed out." He answered,
    "Yes,
But one of these drunken ones is awake, secretly."

Don't say it, Shams of Tabriz. Don't be cruel.
Where shall I find you, my king, again, secretly?

I have not come to the alley of your love to go away

I have not come to the alley of your love to go away.
How can I pray if from my *qibla* I simply go away?

Only a blind man in the dark would not be surprised,
If from that candle with a hundred flames I go away.

What kind of intellect would allow me, a thirsty man,
Asking no help from that prophet of the sea,
   to go away?

I chose the horse of love, riding towards the
   everlasting.
Galloping towards the hair of the beloved, I go away.

Like a falcon by night, and a duck by day, I flap
   my wings.
At dawn, silently praying for him, I secretly go away.

When the blindfold of destiny covers my eyes,
The scent of him makes my eyes open wide and
   go away.

I swear by the dust of the feet of my lord, Shams of
   Tabriz,
He made me who I am with his own hands. Proudly
   I go away.

Free from the world of water and clay, step into my clay

Free from the world of water and clay, step into
    my clay.
I have grown sad and lonely. Rest your hand on
    my heart.

I turned into dark water. I gazed at the road.
Lead me from the road. Transport me to the highest
    heaven.

I was driven crazy by every curl of your tangled hair.
Scatter your locks of disheveled hair into my crazy life.

Whatever harvest I have yields no fruit without you.
Let the stream of your love flow into the field of
    my life.

Do you wish the moth circling my candle to be at
    peace?
Share the fire you possess with my worthy candle.

I am a rope coiled from a hundred curls of your hair.
Coil yourself for a while like a ringlet within my curly
    hair.

The well of Babylon is filled with magic from your
    eyes.
Imprison me in the well of Babylon and cast your
    magic spell.

You said from time immemorial my soul was pregnant.
Drive off evil spirits and place a charm on my load-
    bearing soul.

I pray for a time when you will push away that cloud.
I will say, Come, and rest your face on my full moon.

Shams, the truth of Tabriz, if my soul is at all worthy,
Impress your blessed reunion upon my worthy soul.

To see your face in the early morning is my life

To see your face in the early morning is my life.
Today your lovely face – O God! – steals my heart.

Today in your face, I see another grace.
Today whatever a mad lover does is fine.

Today my critic from yesterday,
After seeing your face, offered an apology.

I wish to borrow a hundred eyes to look at you.
Who will make this loan? Who possesses all eyes?

Today I must go about my business,
Though my heart has been bursting from my chest
    for days.

I blush when I call love human.
I fear God too much to say that God is love.

My eyebrows leaping, my heart beating fast,
As if this good fortune is sneaking up on me.

I'm the fastest dancing tree in all the gardens.
I'm the tree of good fortune. Morning breezes blow
    round my head.

To what sort of tree would you give such leaves?
What sort of stranger lives so near the phoenix?

I whirl in the shadow of your sun,
Even if the blind say, "The shadow is separated from
the tree."

The soul cries, "Such a fiery love!"
When drinking the water of life in your company.

As a vision of you passes through the alleys of my
chest,
My barefoot heart comes to the door and asks, "Where
is my life?"

The earth receives light from your moon,
Like a thousand planets and suns shining in the
firmament.

Shine through the window of my heart like sunshine,
So the sky won't say, "That sun is not friendly."

I was bent like a bow out of pain and sorrow, hitting
the wrong target.
With love, I am like an arrow hitting the right target.

A vision of the land of Tabriz is engraved upon my
heart.
There, the house of blessings, the heart the house
of prayer.

I saw my beauty in your beauty

I saw my beauty in your beauty.
I turned into a mirror for your face.

Flickering with joy, my eyes cannot sleep,
Each dawn, bathing in tears, from reunion with you.

My heart is a woman giving birth at any moment.
She is pregnant with the light of your glory.

Nine months pregnant, when can she rest?
She has no idea of the pain and suffering.

Love, if my blood boils for anyone but you,
Take away my joy and shed my blood freely.

Out of love, head to toe, I turn into living words,
Crying to the heavens, pleading for news of you.

Even if thousands of new worlds are created,
They are like a dot on the face of your beauty.

I drown deeply like a fly in your sweetness,
Too impatient to contemplate your virtues.

Heavenly sky, before Shams, the King of Tabriz,
Bow to the ground to find your own perfection.

I awoke at midnight but couldn't find my heart

I awoke at midnight but couldn't find my heart.
I looked everywhere around the house. Where did
   he go?

When I searched the house, I found the poor thing,
In a corner, crying, whispering the name of God, while
   kneeling.

Listening carefully, I heard him beg for reunion.
While crying, he opened his mouth and began to speak:

"My visible and my invisible are both seen by you.
Inside, I am fire. Outside, smoke and sighs.

Not wishing to find good people broken and defeated,
You add a hundred thousand streams to the stream
   of goodness."

He described the many acts of the king but never said
   the name.
During the darkness of the night, throughout his long
   soliloquy,

All the time, he was whispering, "I never say his
   name –
Though the mere scent of his name is finer than
   incense –

Because I imagine somebody is listening and stealing
  my words.
I don't believe anyone is listening to my tale tonight,
  my king.

It's difficult for me to tell his beautiful name to anyone,
Who doesn't hear his name with proper reverence
  and respect.

And if they hear his name respectfully, then I burn
  with envy."
At that moment he felt exhausted, lost, and confused.

A voice called to him, "Say his name,
Don't worry about others. Say his name boldly.

His name is the key to the wishes of your soul.
Say his name quickly so he will open the door at once."

Anxious about saying his name, the door of the heart
  stayed shut,
Until at last at dawn the sun suddenly appeared.

After a thousand pleas from the voice, the heart cried
  "Tabriz,"
Then he fainted and the threads of the heart
  unraveled.

As I was fainting, the name of Shams al-Din,
That ocean of existence, was engraved upon my heart.

Your eyes intensely beautiful, your face a rose

Your eyes intensely beautiful, your face a rose,
Tell me the truth, what happened to you last night?

Your name is tempting, your trap sweet.
Your wine is fresh, your bread spicy.

If death looks at you, he will see your joy.
Why hide? Wine reveals everything within.

The scent of burning rises from my wailing heart.
The scent of wine rises from your mouth and voice.

Please say something, or leave me alone,
To say one or two words on your behalf.

The beauty of all kings was checkmated,
When just one atom of your immensity was revealed.

Again my eyes saw what no eyes have seen.
Again my master returned ecstatic and drunk.

He kept saying, "You're out of your mind. What
    happened?"
I've lost my mind from sorrow for you and your
    tribulations.

Each dawn, like a late autumn cloud, I rain tears at
    your door.
I wipe the tears from your house with my sleeve.

Whether I travel to the east or west, or up into the sky,
I won't see any sign of life until I see you again.

I was a pious man of the land. I held a pulpit.
Fate made my heart fall in love and dance after you.

I swear to God, I have not drunk the wine of
    this world.
I did not want to be broken. I feared your judgment.

Patience flew from my heart. Reason fled from
    my head.
How far will your reckless drinking drag me?

The black lion of your love tore at my bones.
You were my protection. Why didn't you save me?

Tabriz, once again, say to Shams al-Din,
The two worlds envy you your one noble world.

Where did the handsome beloved go?

Where did the handsome beloved go?
I wonder, where did that tall, shapely cypress tree go?

He spread his light among us like a candle.
Where did he go? So strange, where did he go
    without me?

All day long my heart trembles like a leaf.
All alone at midnight, where did that beloved go?

Go to the road and ask any passing traveler –
That soul-stirring companion, where did he go?

Go to the garden and ask the gardener –
That tall, shapely rose stem, where did he go?

Go to the rooftop and ask the watchman –
That unique sultan, where did he go?

Like a madman, I search in the meadows.
That deer in the meadows, where did he go?

My tearful eyes overflow like a river –
That pearl in the vast sea, where did he go?

All night long, I implore both moon and Venus –
That lovely face, like a moon, where did he go?

If he is mine, why is he with others?
Since he is not here, to what "there" did he go?

If his heart and soul are joined with God,
And he left this realm of earth and water, where did
    he go?

Tell me clearly, Shams of Tabriz,
Of whom it is said, "The sun never dies" – where did
    he go?

**Longing for you, my heart feels more pain
every day**

Longing for you, my heart feels more pain every day,
Though your cruel heart grows weary of me.
You left me, but my longing for you never left.
Truly, my longing for you is more loyal to me
    than you.

You accept me, but rejection is my fear

You accept me, but rejection is my fear.
I am under your protection, but the evil eye is my fear.
The setting of the sun of your beauty is my fear.
The truth is that my own shadow is my fear.

You won't even look at me with a single glance

You won't even look at me with a single glance.
I think it's a sin. You don't want to sin, do you?
While my heart weeps on the roses of your cheeks,
You won't even sigh on the mirror of my heart.

Young man, what if you fell in love like me?

Young man, what if you fell in love like me?
Every day sunk in madness, every night crying.

His memory won't leave me alone for a second.
From his face, I receive hundreds of rays of light.

Separated from friends, giving up the world,
Separated from self, trusting in him.

I spin away from the crowd, like oil from water,
Joined on the outside, separated on the inside.

Freed from desire, but locked in madness,
Yet not the sort of madness any doctor can cure.

If a doctor tasted one drop of my sorrow,
He would flee his work, and tear up his books.

Give up everything. Look for the source of all
    sweetness.
Dissolve in sweetness like a biscuit in milk.

I try to sit and learn but my anxious heart will never be at peace

I try to sit and learn but my anxious heart will never
　　be at peace.
Everyone came and sat, but, even for a moment,
　　my soul will never be at peace.

All who study, at the end, are seated as a master.
I completed the work, did the studying, but will never
　　be at peace.

Whoever hears the clicking of your dry prayer beads,
Until he takes those cries to the court of the Most
　　High, will never be at peace.

Until Solomon is able to reveal the seal of your love to
　　the world,
His throne at the highest place in the heavens will
　　never be at peace.

Whoever gazes on your unruly head and tumble
　　of hair,
His heart, from those tumbling images, will never
　　be at peace.

Whoever, deep in sleep, dreams of your smiling lips,
Awaking, remembering those lips, will never
　　be at peace.

Even sorrow and anger did not keep you from the path,
Seeking a cure for melancholy, you will never
be at peace.

Whoever catches the scent of the rose garden,
Forever dancing towards your rose garden, will never
be at peace.

Once again you are unkind. Remember

Once again you are unkind. Remember.
Not keeping your promise to me. Remember.

Saying we'd be joined until the Resurrection.
Now you're joined with cruelty alone. Remember.

Throughout the dark nights, I was wide-awake.
You left me alone while you slept. Remember.

You whispered in my enemy's ear.
You saw me, and you hid. Remember.

Didn't you say, "I'll be a thorn to your foe"?
Like a rose you bloomed with him. Remember.

I grabbed your robe and you pulled away.
You did that and you left. Remember.

I used to reproach you, but I did it softly.
Your reproaches to me are loud and harsh. Remember.

You fell many times. I held your hand.
You will fall once again. Remember.

**I wish to devote my life to him but I won't tell
you his name**

I wish to devote my life to him but I won't tell you
    his name.
May that day when I can no longer find him be black!

I will quickly become a disgraced figure throughout
    the city,
If tomorrow I wait at the door of my heart while he
    walks the alley.

I said, "Beloved, with the face of the moon! Look for
    me, sometime."
Out of pain, I wash my face with my heart's blood.

He said, "I found you but you were not home."
O God! He talks such nonsense to my face.

One day, I swear to God, while reciting ghazals,
    I will die,
As my life grows thin as a strand of hair from
    weeping.

I cure my pain with suffering

I cure my pain with suffering,
And make my work easier with patience.

I pull the foot of my soul out of the mud,
And bequeath my heart and soul to lovers.

I am a moth burned in the candle of eternity,
Serving the royal candle of the king.

I invite love into my burned heart,
Having but one heart to sacrifice for love.

If the lower self is like a cat that meows,
I know how to lure that cat into a sack.

Whoever is sadly shaking his head,
I pull into the circle and make him whirl.

Since sadness comes from not having love,
I make his soul fall in love with love itself.

What is love? Absolute thirst.
I try to speak about the fountain of life.

Since I cannot find the words, I remain silent.
Whatever I cannot put into words, I do.

I swear to God, I'm not running from the pain of your love

I swear to God, I'm not running from the pain of
    your love.
If you want to take my life, I won't resist, I won't
    resist.

I swear to God, I'm holding a cup in my hand, if you
    don't return
Until the day of resurrection, I won't pour it, I won't
    drink it.

My dawn is your moonlike face, my night your
    black hair.
I swear to God, without your face and hair, I won't
    sleep, I won't wake up.

From your glory, I am glorious. From your guidance,
    I am guided.
I am of the line of Abraham. I stand within the stinging
    flames of fire.

Give me water from the jar. Love does not just last a
    day or two.
Your pain is like prayer and fasting, both necessary
    and required.

I swear to God, a branch of a tree that does not have
   your blessing,
No matter how much water I pour, will turn into a
   piece of tinder.

Fly away, heart, toward the heaven above, strong and
   supreme,
Before the throne of the Almighty no servant exists
   like you.

Everyone worships God during times of trouble,
But you are present day and night, like the sky,
   judicious and wise.

I can never fully describe the pride of Tabriz.
What to do, how to sift the powder of this aromatic
   cure?

Even if I lose my sight and mind and life, don't go

Even if I lose my sight and mind and life, don't go.
I'd rather look at you than at all of them, don't go.

The sun and the sky are under your protection.
Even if the sky and the shining stars vanish, don't go.

The roughest of your words are purer than mercy.
Even if pure eloquence vanishes, don't go.

All believers fear the end of the world.
My fear is losing you, my king of faith, don't go.

Don't go, and if you go, take my life with you.
If you don't take me from this earth with you, don't go.

With you, the whole world is a rose garden.
Even if the beautiful rose garden disappears in autumn,
    don't go.

Don't leave me alone. To leave, you would need a heart
    of stone.
Even if stones are turned into finest rubies, don't go.

When the atom pleads with the shining sun, don't go.
When the slave pleads with the king, don't go.

You are the water of life and we are all fish,
Swimming in your mercy and kindness and beauty,
    don't go.

The scroll of my heart unrolls to eternity.
Written from the beginning to the end are the words
 "don't go."

If I weren't afraid of tiring you, I'd recite a hundred
 verses.
Even better than a hundred, I'd recite eighteen
 thousand, don't go.

My friend, all alone, without a friend, don't leave me

My friend, all alone, without a friend, don't leave me.
Don't pass me by, don't leave me, don't leave me.

The soul of your servant came under your protection,
In the midst of separation, without protection, don't
    leave me.

You are the physician, perhaps the Jesus of our time,
Don't go, I'm very sick, don't leave me.

You told me, "You are my companion in the cave."
It's so lonely in the cave, don't leave me.

To you, separation for one night seems so small.
Ask me about small and big and don't leave me.

Don't throw a small fire into my heart.
Fire never burns in small amounts, don't leave me.

I am breathless. But one more time,
Listen to me, this time, don't leave me.

Since you went away, I am weeping, as you know

Since you went away, I am weeping, as you know.
I am eager to see you once again, as you know.

Since your love entered my heart and settled there,
All patience and peace have vanished, as you know.

The rose was hidden. The nightingale flew from my
    meadow.
I became weary of the pain of the thorns, as you know.

From endless wailing, my white falcon turned into
    an owl.
Among the mountains, I am a mere starling, as you
    know.

I was a ripe, smiling pomegranate on your lips of agate.
Now I am like a flame of fire, as you know.

Your secret remains hidden in my heart,
Never to be put into words, as you know.

Your pomegranate of love was Shams of Tabriz.
He led me to the martyr's gallows, as you know.

I said to the physician, "Please find a cure."

I said to the physician, "Please find a cure."
Taking my pulse, with wisdom and learning,
He said, "What hurts? Show me."
So I took his hand and placed it on my aching heart.

For Majnun's health

For Majnun's health,
Physician, recite a magic spell.

As a cure for madness,
Drip opium in his wine.

Since there's no cure, I seek ecstasy,
And search for true beauty.

Look into my heart, full of sorrow.
Wine bearer, bring that ruby cup, full of blood.

The mind, striving for the highest,
Never satisfied, bows to the lowest.

Drunken mystics don't need a penny,
To buy a silver moon and a gold sun.

Ask Majnun about sublime love,
To find what's hidden inside his head.

The heresies of love
Break a hundred thousand rules.

Morning breeze, please go on my behalf,
Kindly, to the hidden pearl within the sea.

Even if he angrily answers, "No I won't,"
Beg him to give life to my lifeless clay.

Shams of Tabriz! The Moses of our time!
Don't keep Aaron waiting endlessly.

The physician for incurable pain, where is he?

The physician for incurable pain, where is he?
The companion on the road without end, where is he?

If this is reason, what is madness?
If this is soul, the beloveds, where are they?

The lamp of eternity illuminating the world,
Possessing neither faith nor lack of faith, where is it?

The sea of everlasting life is full of pearls.
The pearl of humanity within the sea, where is it?

Everyone is wearing the cloaks of humble servants.
Among the slaves, the king, where is he?

No one living in this world is free from illness.
The physician of love, his shop, where is it?

Hapless thoughts of the powerful have exhausted
The intellect. But humility, where is he?

The perfect idol ran from the house of idols.
For the perfectly made, the measure, where is it?

Why make a *qibla* of these questions and answers?
Ask instead, the lesson of the silent ones, where is it?

The tulips bloom in dry soil when they see your face

The tulips bloom in dry soil when they see your face.
The sour grapes turn to honey when they see
     your lips.

Last night I dreamed I was reading your book of love.
My soul grew crazed from reading a single chapter.

The paradox of the two worlds turns so sweet,
When all your sugar is poured into a single cake.

Face of the sun, shed your rays on the bodies of
     the grapes,
So the bodies of all creatures below may be filled
     with sweetness.

Being free from the self is as easy as separating thread
     from a spool,
When the thread has grown restless from being bound
     to the spool.

The body is like a honey melon needing to release its
     flavor.
You must slice open the melon if you wish to know its
     true value.

You have not yet seen love's courtyard,
Dancing heads, wrapped in turbans, swirling in
     a torrent.

I was lovesick when I went to the physician of both
   worlds,
The pulse of my pounding heart held in his hand like
   a glass of wine.

I said to him, "Shams al-Din, the pride of Tabriz!
How can my wound ever be cured without you?"

One day as I was passing by the tavern

One day as I was passing by the tavern,
I took off my rough cloak.
Everyone was looking in different directions.
I alone was looking into my own vision.

Without a cup, without wine, I am happy

Without a cup, without wine, I am happy.
Each morning I glow, each night I am happy.
They keep saying, "You have no future."
Without a future, I am happy.

Love lured me into the alley of the tavern

Love lured me into the alley of the tavern.
The wandering beloved saw me and gave a sign.

I followed after him, the beloved wanderer.
In an instant he showed his face once more.

I was astonished by this polestar of the world.
With one glance, he made my entire soul come alive.

Suddenly a deer of many colors appeared.
From the splendor of his beauty, the sun and moon
    wept.

That deer with his beautiful musk traveled to Tabriz,
Transformed into Baghdad by his visions and
    knowledge.

Whoever bowed to him as a follower,
He chose for happiness and favor in the world.

Whoever said, I am perfect and beyond compare,
He left lost, melancholy, and outcast.

The sultan of knowledge was the keeper of secrets,
Speaking of all the glorious secrets of eternity.

When Shams of Tabriz opened his wings of love,
Even the loyal angel Gabriel ran after him.

What better cure than madness?

What better cure than madness?
Pull up a hundred anchors with madness!

Sometimes the intellect gives rise to apostasy.
Have you ever seen doubt caused by madness?

When your pain grows fat, go mad.
Your pain will grow thin from madness.

In the tavern where the mad ones go,
Quickly grab a cup of madness.

Are the insane so poor and miserable?
They are kings and emperors from madness.

Happy, and joyful, and victorious,
The entire army of Persia, from madness.

You may ascend to heaven like Christ,
If you are borne aloft by wings of madness.

Shams of Tabriz! To find your love,
I opened a hundred doors of madness.

When hung over, with a headache, longing for love

When hung over, with a headache, longing for love,
The wine steward arrives with the red wine of love.

When the joyful drum rouses the army of love,
"We have granted thee victory!" blares the trumpet
    of love.

When poison in the mouths of lovers turns to honey,
Sugar rises through the reed flutes of love.

When a cloud begins to cover the moon,
The cloud is set on fire by the lightning of love.

On the road through the burning desert sands,
Like a clap of thunder cries the wine steward of love.

Wine steward! Pour wine over the heads of everyone,
Or toast the rising and the cresting of love.

When Shams of Tabriz shines from the tower of truth,
The arc of the wave rises from the ocean of love.

When day is done, join the wine drinkers, all night

When day is done, join the wine drinkers, all night.
Join with friends and strangers, from night until day.

Don't stray, fair Joseph, too far from the eyes of Jacob.
Make this night the Night of Power, be a lamp
  amid grief.

If I am far from you, be merciful. If I am naked,
  be my garment.
If I am weak, be my strength. If I am in pain,
  be my cure.

If I have no faith, be my faith. If I sin, be my
  forgiveness.
If I am blind, be compassionate. Be my heaven and my
  paradise.

To bring forth an angel, beat the soul's drum.
To send away a devil, hurl a shooting star at Satan.

You are the sea and the world is a fish. You are in time
  and eternal.
If you wish for the fish to live, be for them the water
  of life.

Dark night would be so joyful if the moon would
　　join me.
Rise, O moon, and shine, for the night travelers of
　　the soul.

Be still, anxious heart. Speak no more of good and evil.
The secret is revealed in his presence. Close your
　　mouth and be hidden.

Send me your soul's wine as a token of your love

Send me your soul's wine as a token of your love,
As a sign you are able to find me without any signs,

As a reminder that you shine like the moon every
    evening,
From the heart's cloud pouring down the rain of life.

Such amazing raindrops falling from the language
    of love,
So many roses upon roses bloom, so many thorns
    upon thorns.

Among the roses and the thorns my heart is like a
    drunken nightingale.
At dawn you magically reveal the secret at the heart
    of love.

I cry a thousand cries of ecstasy from drinking love's
    wine,
Like a harp crying, unaware of the music I'm playing,

From the moment I beheld the goblet of your love,
I was empty one moment, full the next.

Why are you passing me among the crowd like a cup?
Yet you are not revealing to them the candle's light.

Ask me, who is this candle, Shams al-Din,
Who awakened the land of Tabriz with his light?

**Since you are drunk with me, over a hangover,
why worry?**

Since you are drunk with me, over a hangover,
    why worry?
Since you are my deer, over a lion, why worry?

Since I am your moon, why think about months
    and years?
Since I fill you with pleasure, over fears, why worry?

Since you are a field of sugar, why such a sour face?
Since you tamed the steed of love, over a mule,
    why worry?

Since I am warm with you, why are your sighs so cold?
Since you are above the heavens, over dry and wet,
    why worry?

You heard my joyous singing. You saw my healing
    remedies.
Since you saw my nimble dancing, over this snake's
    coil, why worry?

Why is your face so rigid? Why do you fear
    annihilation?
Since you are holding the pearl, over losing it,
    why worry?

Joseph, no one can resist the grip of your hand
 and thumb.
Since all Egypt is drunk with you, over going deaf
 and blind, why worry?

When you are in a cave with the beloved, you turn into
 a lamp.
Since you are a mystic with the sword of Ali, over a
 dagger, why worry?

You took all the gardens and trees and are drinking the
 nectar and sap.
Since all the doors are shut, over lock and key,
 why worry?

Since you saw your rising and falling tides, your wings
 and feathers,
Since you saw your power and dignity, over small
 things, why worry?

O soul of soul of souls, you shelter the souls of your
 guests.
O king of kings, over a mere prince, why worry?

Be as silent as a fish and dive into the ocean of joy.
Since you are deep within the ocean, over fires,
 why worry?

Who am I? What am I thinking? Serve the wine!

Who am I? What am I thinking? Serve the wine!
Pour from that soul-reviving cup into my soul. Serve
the wine!

Consoler of lovers, place the soulful cup in my hand,
Hide it far from the lips of strangers. Serve the wine!

Give bread to the children and the hungry and needy.
Put the lover of breadcrumbs to bed in the corner.
Serve the wine!

Soul of the soul of the soul of the soul, I have not come
for bread.
Get up! Don't be stingy at the royal banquet. Serve
the wine!

First, place the moon's cup in the palm of the wise
old man.
When he gets drunk, move on to the other drinkers.
Serve the wine!

Walk confidently. Don't be shy. Drinkers feel no shame.
If you feel shame, pour a cup of wine on your shame.
Serve the wine!

Get up, wine steward! Come here! You enemy of shame
and modesty,
Until fortune begins to smile on me, come closer,
smiling. Serve the wine!

He makes my soul drunk without wine.
Where is he?

He makes my soul drunk without wine. Where is he?
He releases my heart and soul. Where is he?

I swear to drink to his health alone.
I broke my oath and vow for him. Where is he?

All souls are crying for him at dawn.
His sorrow pulled me by my roots. Where is he?

How amazing that such a dear soul has no refuge!
His refuge is within my body. Where is he?

Behind his flirting glances is longing.
His glances conceal such hurt. Where is he?

The light of my heart was veiled and visions appeared.
He quietly drew a veil over my heart. Where is he?

When the intellect got drunk, how and why no longer
    mattered.
He was drunk and free from asking how and why.
    Where is he?

Why is night-blind sorrow wrapping about me?

Why is night-blind sorrow wrapping about me?
Is sorrow blind, or does it think that I am blind?
I am above the heavens, reflected in water and clay.
Has anyone ever stolen a star from the water?

When I fall into the chaos of night

When I fall into the chaos of night,
I make waves in the ocean of night.

Not wishing to sleep, running from sleep,
I keep watch throughout the night.

My heart full of light, my soul full of purity,
I am the slave and servant of the master of night.

Night is the veil over the invisible observer.
How can day compare with night?

You think the night is like a black pot,
You have not tasted the *halva* of night.

Night pulled my hand from work and trade,
Holding my hand until dawn pulled the foot of night.

The road is long so I ride quickly,
Through the length and breadth of night.

If day is a time for marketing and trade,
A different joy is found in the market of night.

Shams al-Din, you are the pride of Tabriz,
You are the envy of day and the desire of night.

Tonight sleep ran from my eyes and mind

Tonight sleep ran from my eyes and mind.
Seeing my broken heart, it ran away.

Sleep saw my dry and broken heart.
As my skewered heart had lost its salt, it ran away.

Poor, wretched sleep, in the paws of love,
Wounded, and full of anguish, it ran away.

Love, like a crocodile, opened its mouth.
Sleep, like a fish, slipped into the water, and ran away.

When sleep saw the brutal battlefield,
Without wasting a moment, in a hurry, it ran away.

My moon arose at night, as did this sleep.
Like a shadow, from the sun, it ran away.

When sleep saw the cycle of reawakening,
Like a sparrow, from the eagle, it ran away.

When the phoenix of good fortune at last appeared,
With wings wide open, this crow ran away.

Love asked a single question of sleep.
Stuck for an answer, it ran away.

Sleep shut the door of the six directions.
When God unlocked the door, it ran away.

Shams of Tabriz! Dreaming of you, sleep,
Chasing illusions, not the truth, ran away.

If you can't find me, ask the dark night

If you can't find me, ask the dark night.
Night is close with lovers and hears their cries
    and tears.

Is the night not full with thousands of hints of lovers?
Observing their tears and wan faces, wasted and thin.

Like clouds shedding tears, like mountains enduring
    time,
Like water kneeling in prayer, like dirt humbly
    scattering.

All grief outside the garden is but a tiny thorn.
Inside the garden are roses and lovers and running
    fountains.

When you pass the garden wall and step onto the
    green grass,
You break into a prayer of gratitude and bow in
    thanksgiving.

Thanks be to God for taking away the injuries of
    autumn,
For making the earth blossom and the spring so
    spring-like.

Thousands of naked branches festooned with flowering
    buds,
Thousands of Acacia trees freed from their thorns.

What does the scholar know of the sweet taste of a
  lover's sorrow?
A horse unskilled in galloping can never ride into
  battle.

Your brother and your father and your mother are
  all beloved,
Woven together as one, and united in community.

When a thousand bodies fall in salty land, they turn
  into salt.
All bodies are the same, whether from Merv or
  Bukhara.

Don't pull at the old mule's bridle of speech.
Look to those thirsty for heaven when the time comes
  to speak.

Sleep follows after you to take away logic and intellect

Sleep follows after you to take away logic and intellect.
Where does a madman sleep? What does he know
   of night?

Neither day nor night exists in the path of the
   madman.
Whatever he himself has, he knows, he knows.

Day and night exist because of the circling of the sky.
The madman in his world has no circling sky.

The eyes in his head sleep but he is all eyes without
   a head.
With the eyes of his soul he can read the runes of all
   that came before.

If you are seeking madness, turn into a bird or a fish.
If you are a friend of sleep, madness will stay far
   from you.

Turn into a wandering sleepwalker in love with the
   beloved,
Until the problem is untangled by the spreading of
   his curls.

The madman is a special creature, pregnant with soul.
When his eyes gaze at the beloved, he will give birth
   quickly.

If you want an explanation, seek Shams, the King
    of Truth,
The whole world is Tabriz, filled by him with
    new light.

Moon, on such a night be moonlike. Don't sleep!

Moon, on such a night be moonlike. Don't sleep!
Whirl around us, like the circling heavens. Don't sleep!
A waking moon is the lamp of the world.
For tonight, keep your lamp lit. Don't sleep!

Last night a ravishing moon came to me

Last night a ravishing moon came to me.
I said, "Go away! You're not meant to be here tonight."
Walking away, he said, "How crazy.
Good fortune comes and you don't even open
the door."

Water washed away all my poems and songs

Water washed away all my poems and songs.
Floods washed away the only clothes I wore.
My piety, my good and bad, were revealed
In the moonlight and vanished in the moonlight.

The silver-bodied moon poked his head through the sky

The silver-bodied moon poked his head through
　　the sky,
Motioning towards me with the long sleeves of
　　his robe.

Like the eyes of the dead, my eyes are transfixed
　　by him.
From the wine of his love, my soul leaves my body.

Beneath the dark curls of his hair, a hundred
　　resurrections,
In the bright circle of his face, all human suffering.

The soul's bird in its cage plucks its feathers and
　　wings,
Twisting the bars of its cage, desiring the twists of that
　　hair.

A phoenix flew through the sky, casting its shadow on
　　my head.
I screamed, "Go away. Don't cover the face of that
　　sweet scent."

The phoenix replied, "You miserable man,
You ungrateful student, you run from good fortune."

I told him, "You are the curtain between me and my
    friend.
I want to see his face or my soul will never be at peace."

Curious, the phoenix turned his head to look at the
    moon,
And grew even more insane than I, infatuated by
    his beauty.

Prince, drunk, Master, drunk, Soul, drunk, Body,
    drunk,
From the Lord Shams al-Din, the King of Tabriz, and
    from me.

The flame of moonlight moves with grace

The flame of moonlight moves with grace.
The gorgeous angel of paradise moves with grace.

The clothing of night turns to white,
As that faraway moon moves with grace.

Nighttime revelers reel from good news,
As the boy bringing wine, at dawn, moves with grace.

My soul burns like the wood of the aloe tree,
As that mine full of crystals moves with grace.

Look at the gorgeous angel, one more time,
Creating joy a hundredfold, she moves with grace.

The enemy of the lover's patience,
Into the lover's wound, moves with grace.

I devote my soul to Solomon.
He moves towards the ant with grace.

Gaze only into the faces of lovers,
As that king of devotion moves with grace.

Among the bodies of the living, Shams of Tabriz,
Like the blast of a trumpet, moves with grace.

You are a moon that in the sky cannot be held

You are a moon that in the sky cannot be held.
You are water that in the River Oxus cannot be held.

You are a pearl that is bigger than the sea.
You are a mountain that on a plateau cannot be held.

What magic spell can I recite, king of the angels?
Who by bottles and magic spells cannot be held?

You are Layli, yet because of your jealous lover,
In the corner of Majnun's mind you cannot be held.

You are a sun. Your cloak is the heart's light.
You are wrapped in fine satin that cannot be held.

You are a student of the physician who revives souls.
Within the reasoning of Plato you cannot be held.

You are a potion that cannot be found in any trove.
What trove is that? That in logic cannot be held.

The enemy says: "Thus he is like this and that."
You are incomparable, so within "who" or "what," you
    cannot be held.

You were like this and that, within the belly of the world.
Then you could have been held, but now you cannot
    be held.

Don't recite into just any ear. Be silent!
Within just any ear madly in love you cannot be held.

O Moon, any night you shine, I throw myself at your feet

O Moon, any night you shine, I throw myself at
    your feet,
Begging you not to hasten into the darkness, my
    beloved.

For travelers by night, you are their eyes and their
    lamp.
For travelers to heaven, you are their fire and their
    water.

In this heavenly inn, turning in a sacred circle,
Perhaps destiny will lead you to find my moon.

He is the soul of the world and the soul has no location.
If you are full of virtue, walk towards him, filled with
    charity.

Tell him: "I have a message for you, since you create
    souls,
Please respond, as I know your answer will be full
    of mercy.

You have won a thousand chips and the game has just
    begun.
You have torn a thousand curtains yet you are still
    hidden.

My heart is filled with wounds and hidden
   lamentations.
You play my heart's rabab with your knowing hands.

My heart is like a rabab and my body like a tavern.
Play the rabab and whirl like a drunk about the tavern.

Everyone is drunk, drinking wine from your cup,
You're drunk, too. But which wine are you drinking?"

Where is the seashore, O Heart, forever drowning?
Where is the unseen fire, always and forever burning?

If the moon that shines in the night veils himself

If the moon that shines in the night veils himself,
He hides his face but where does he hide his scent?

If he covers his face and his scent,
His heavenly jar can be drunk in a hundred ways.

That runaway moon shows up behind the house
Yet my crazy heart is afraid in a hundred ways.

Though sorrow is not my friend, it tells me secrets.
Telling the bird of my heart where it hides its net.

The sky has never seen such a moon, not even in its dreams

The sky has never seen such a moon, not even in
    its dreams.
No water could ever extinguish the fire of its light.

Look at my body and look at my soul.
From his cup of love, my body is ruined, my soul
    drunk.

The tavern keeper became my heart's companion.
Love turned my blood into wine and burned my heart.

As my eyes fill with the image of his face, a voice
    resounds,
"Well done, cup. Praise to you, wine."

Looking into the ocean of love,
My heart suddenly dove in, calling, "Find me!"

The face of the sun is Shams, the glory of Tabriz.
Our hearts, like clouds, trail after him.

O you, who rose from my soul, where is your house?

Oh you, who rose from my soul, where is your house?
My shining moon, where is your house?

Strong and powerful, hidden in the body, seen in
    the heart,
My seen and unseen, where is your house?

You say, "A longing heart is the house of kings."
My heart is anxious, dear friend, where is your house?

The moon's shadow is a midwife, when will she find
    the moon?
Tell me, Moon, I don't know, where is your house?

I saw the moon's reflection, whirling through a
    hundred houses.
Free me from all of this searching, where is your
    house?

From the fire of love, cold grows warm

From the fire of love, cold grows warm.
From the light of love, rocks grow soft.
Don't be hard on the sins of lovers.
The wine of love has made them bold.

I pulled you out of one fire

I pulled you out of one fire
To push you into another.

My heart gave birth to you, like speech.
I swallowed you as if you were the last word.

You are with me, without knowing who I am.
I am magic and I cast a spell on you.

That no evil might befall your beautiful face,
I pinched your ears until they hurt.

Your destiny grows younger every day,
The palm of my hand gives nourishment to you.

Lovers are aflame with a hidden fire

Lovers are aflame with a hidden fire,
Revealing good and evil in the light of their fire.

A royal seal is engraved on lovers' hearts,
A royal throne surrounded by flames of fire.

Rays of sunlight shine in lovers' windows.
I am as delirious as an atom of dust in the blazing fire.

Welcome, lovers, to the banquet of love,
Fire-eaters dining on a feast of fire.

The sky mirrors the fiery flames,
As far as the eye can see, all the stars are on fire.

Only look for warmth from the burning fire inside you

Only look for warmth from the burning fire inside you.
The heart is not lit by flames from any other fire.

You must be sick with pain for the unseen king
   to arrive.
Opening the door of the heart and gently asking,
   "How are you?"

The scent of musk, the hair of the fair beloved –
These treasures are rare. They are not found
   everywhere.

Unless you die, your soul will never turn into an angel.
Unless you are killed, your love will never be as red
   as blood.

His love says to you, "Either I go, or you."
Don't remain still, even if you are moving without
   moving.

Only a wounded heart knows the secret of the soul,
So the self stays free of blame and you're not a
   wild horse.

Sorrow squeezes you, separating you from your self,
So light may rain down on you from the azure skies.

If you sit with pain, you will always see your beloved.
Poor, miserable thing, why look for magic remedies?

Tabriz, you come to life as the truth of Shams arrives.
You will always be blessed, now and forever.

My turban, my robe, and my head, all three together

My turban, my robe, and my head, all three together,
Are worth less than a penny.
Have you heard my name in the world?
I am nobody. I am nobody. I am nobody.

Sorrow turned the heart into a scholar

Sorrow turned the heart into a scholar,
Like a hard piece of silver in a fire temple, the scholar.

In hopes of your mercy and generosity,
To arrive at the end of his long journey, the scholar.

Filled with visions of you on love's road,
Weary, lovesick, and tired of his road, the scholar.

What is the harm in a friend's compassion?
If he finds there strength and nourishment,
   the scholar?

When you serve such a cup of insanity,
How will he ever remain standing, the scholar?

Will your sense of justice and honor
Allow him to die senselessly from sorrow, the scholar?

Will the true sun, spreading heat and light,
Allow him to freeze and sink into depression,
   the scholar?

Your mercy pulled him toward the school of love,
Where he began to stir from your lessons, the scholar.

Struggling with the four elements, have mercy on him,
Until illuminated by a ray of light from above,
    the scholar.

Having much to say, but afraid of tiring you,
He keeps his lips sealed in this temple, the scholar.

Even if you're not a scholar, study with me

Even if you're not a scholar, study with me.
Even if you're not a musician, sing with me.

Even if you're rich, you will be poor in love.
Even if you're a lord, come be a slave with me.

One candle from this circle lights a hundred candles.
Even if you're dead, come back to life with me.

When you walk freely, the light will shine on you,
Your whole body, like a rose, smiling with me.

Put on these torn rags to behold the light-hearted.
Throw out your satin and wear these rags with me.

When the seed is scattered, it grows into a tree.
When you know this secret, come be scattered
    with me.

Shams, the truth of Tabriz, says to the rosebud of
    the heart,
"When your eyes are open wide, come, and watch
    with me."

Within love is the alchemy of sunrise

Within love is the alchemy of sunrise.
Within a cloud, a hundred thousand bolts of lightning.
Within me is an ocean of his splendor.
Within him, all creation is drowning.

Love can't be found in science or knowledge, books or paper

Love can't be found in science or knowledge, books or paper.
What others say is never the path of lovers.

The branches of love are primeval. The roots of love endless.
This tree with no trunk touches neither soil nor heavenly sky.

I abandoned logic and curbed all my striving.
The majesty of love transcends intellect and nature.

You eagerly worship your own longing.
When you are transformed into the beloved, all longing vanishes.

You are a sailor sailing on the boat of fear and hope.
When sailor and boat are annihilated only drowning remains.

Shams of Tabriz, you are the ocean and the pearl.
Your life is full of the mystery of the Creator.

As lover nears lover, their chains break apart

As lover nears lover, their chains break apart.
As they grow mad, their thoughts break apart.

What is the sin in walking in the heat of love?
In the fire of love, all sins break apart.

The young man's feelings erupt like fire,
As the old man's cloak of piety breaks apart.

A hundred hidden veils concealed in the eyes,
From an arrow shot by the bow of the eyebrows break
    apart.

As the bird of the heart of the lover is hatched,
Beneath its talons all hesitation breaks apart.

This world is like tar, where all feet are stuck,
When the fire of love erupts, the tar breaks apart.

Shams, the truth of Tabriz, is the king and the prince.
Because of that prince, the robe of patience breaks
    apart.

If you're not in love, you're allowed, sleep on

If you're not in love, you're allowed, sleep on.
Leave all the love and sorrow for me, sleep on.

In the sunlight of his sorrow, we are specks of dust,
If you don't feel his passion in your heart, sleep on.

Seeking to be close to him, seeking water to drink,
If you're not worried about finding him, sleep on.

The path of love is beyond the seventy-two creeds.
If your love and your religion are full of lies, sleep on.

Our breakfast is his wine, our supper his sweetness.
If you're worried about food for supper, sleep on.

You're pursuing alchemy, I'm already melted copper.
If your life is devoted to studying alchemy, sleep on.

Like a drunk, I'm falling down and getting up.
The night has passed, it's time for prayer, sleep on.

My destiny has kept me awake, you, young man, go on,
Sleep has breathed on you, now sleep is your destiny,
    sleep on.

I'm being held in the hands of love. What can I do?
Since you hold your life in your own hands, sleep on.

I'm full of sorrow. You're full of food.
After eating, you need lots of sleep, sleep on.

I've lost all hope in my mind and in my head.
Your young mind is filled with hope, sleep on.

I rip off my robe of words. I let go of speech.
If you don't wish to be naked, I'll give you my robe,
    sleep on.

Sit with lovers and always seek love

Sit with lovers and always seek love.
Stay far from anyone who is not in love.

Don't pursue a lover covered with a proper veil.
Pursue a lover whose face is open and unveiled.

Gaze at a face that reflects his face.
Gaze at a face that glows like the sun.

As the sun kisses both his cheeks,
The king is checkmated, the moon bows.

Written in his curls: "I worship you."
Burning through his eyes: "I seek you."

Without blood or veins, his body is like a dream.
Inside and outside, all is milk and honey.

He always holds his beloved close.
He loses the scent of the earth in his scent.

He is morning without dawn, evening without sunset,
Essence without substance, life without sorrow.

Does the sun need to borrow its light from the sky?
Does the rose need to borrow its scent from jasmine?

Be as wordless as a fish and as clear as the sea.
Soon you will benefit from the treasure of the pearl.

I whisper something in your ear, but don't tell anyone.
Who is this perfection? Shams al-Din, the pride
    of Tabriz.

I swear by love even if love is full of baits and traps

I swear by love even if love is full of baits and traps,
I will go on a hundred journeys from Byzantium
    to Syria.

I do not swear by right and wrong,
I swear by the love that is beyond right and wrong.

I swear by the love that is gentler than the purest
    spirit.
For lovers, love is their food and drink.

Is love not the fire where my soul lives?
Is love not the crucible where my coins turn to gold?

Is love not a wine bearer and my soul drunk night
    and day?
Is my body not a cup for that primordial wine?

Love came to my side and put a cup in my hand,
And thousands of me became the slaves of love.

My soul and love tell each other thousands of secrets,
Secrets that cannot be expressed in rhyming words.

Bring a bottle of new wine to the empty house.
Even the melting lover is not yet cooked without love.

Beyond thought, joyfully draw close to love,
Beyond logic and the suffering of the world.

When love and I lose ourselves in wine,
The king of Tabriz appears. Salaam, Shams al-Din!

Why should a lover fear shame or disgrace?

Why should a lover fear shame or disgrace?
Love is its own perfect kingdom, desiring only itself.

The panther of love doesn't fear this world's colors
    or scents.
The sea monster of selflessness doesn't fear swallowing
    hell's waters.

The lover was so drunk from that wine,
The cup could no longer taste its own wine.

When a drop fell on a mountain, the dirt
Cried a thousand cries of turmoil and revolt.

What do you know of the cup of love when your heart
    is delicate glass?
What do you know of the trap of love when your heart
    is a trapped bird?

I don't talk of the sea's purity when its waves are full
    of foam.
You are as restless as a drop of mercury held in the
    palm of a hand.

Why be guilty about such joy, why so dark and
    melancholy?
What is the crime in vinegar swallowing crystals
    of sugar?

Curses on the vinegar, and on the vinegar merchant,
If he doesn't drink the pure syrup during such
    dark days.

Look at me, the least important person at this
    celebration.
I'm so lost in ecstasy, I can't tell the difference between
    high and low.

If there's no trace of love in his heart

If there's no trace of love in his heart,
Cover him like an angry cloud over the moon.

Dry tree, don't grow in that garden.
Poor thing, left without the shade of this tree.

Even if you're a pearl, don't separate from this love.
Love is your father and your family.

On the path of lovers, a deadly illness strikes,
Each day more painful than the last.

If you see the blush of love in someone's face,
Know that he is no longer merely mortal.

If you see a reed flute, bent by love, grab it.
Squeeze the reed until you taste the sweetest sugar.

Shams of Tabriz lures you into his trap.
Don't look to the left or right, you can't resist.

Take these breadcrumbs but my soul will never be broken

Take these breadcrumbs but my soul will never be
    broken.
My love may wander in exile but will never be hurt.

Since I am his cloak, he will never be naked.
Since I am his cure, he will never be ill.

Lifted by me, how could he ever be brought low?
The black stone turned into a pearl will never be
    coarse.

The *qibla* of lovers will never be turned into a ruin.
The book of silence will never be torn into thirty parts.

With so many tears, my eyes are like a wine bearer,
But without his intoxicating eyes, the wine bearer has
    no tavern.

The lover grows ill but will never die.
Even if the moon grows thin, he will never turn into
    a star.

Be silent! Don't be filled with sorrow.
The spirit that falls in love will never do wrong.

Tomorrow I visit the shop of the tailor of lovers

Tomorrow I visit the shop of the tailor of lovers,
Full of melancholy, my robe a thousand yards long.

Someone is snipped away, and I am sewn to another,
Stitched together, forever, seamlessly.

I give my heart to him, all my life,
As the tailor's miraculous hands stitch with silk thread.

If I give my heart, separation may tear my robe apart,
Wounded by the precious scissors of "Get ye down all
from here."

Amazed by his adding and subtracting,
Fascinated by his fixing and erasing, my heart changes
colors.

My heart is a tablet, where he records his
measurements,
Lines and numbers, sizes and names.

What if he multiplies me by two, like a number?
What if he multiplies me by himself!

Now that I am multiplied, come see the pieces,
Divided and scattered like drops in the sea.

In his algebra, opposites equal each other.
Be silent! Thinking shreds before these marvels.

Didn't I tell you last night, "Your beautiful face is beyond compare"

Didn't I tell you last night, "Your beautiful face is
  beyond compare.
The moon, jealous of your beauty, was torn in two.

Today you are a hundred times grander. You were a
  guard, now a king.
You turned into Joseph and the glorious light of
  Mohammad.

Tonight I worship you, my angel. Tomorrow you will
  surpass speech.
Tomorrow debates about you by earth and sky will
  come to nothing.

Tonight I hold onto you. I am your servant and slave.
Tomorrow even the king will faint away and heaven rip
  off its robes."

Suddenly a strong wind rises. No roofs or doors
  remain.
Flies can't fly away. They are like elephants without
  feet.

Once again through the wind shine goodness and light,
Each atom smiling in the light of the morning sun.

These atoms learn from the beautiful face of the sun –
A hundred ravishing atoms that never existed before.

I tested everyone but didn't find anyone sweeter than you

I tested everyone but didn't find anyone sweeter
    than you.
When I dove into the sea, I never found a pearl
    like you.

I opened the vat and tested thousands of wines.
Except for your strong wine, no wine came to my lips
    and mind.

Is it so strange that roses and jasmine are laughing at
    my heart?
Since such gentle jasmine as you has not come into
    my arms?

Pursuing you, I left behind desire for two or
    three days.
What's the point of desire when satisfaction
    never arrives?

For two or three days I was a slave in your kingdom.
In all the world, I never found another king I wished
    to serve.

My mind said, "Fly towards those traveling to heaven."
Why sit with a broken leg waiting for a traveler
    to come?

When the heart's dove flew towards your roof from
    my body,
Like a nightingale, I began to lament. Where has my
    dove gone?

Looking for the heart's dove, I flew into the air like
    a falcon.
No phoenix or bird of paradise ever seemed as fine
    to me.

O restless body, go away, you and that sorrowful heart.
Until I free myself from you both, my new heart will
    never come.

**In all of love has there ever been such a lover
as you?**

In all of love has there ever been such a lover as you?
Out of desire for you, even kings wear tattered robes.

Solomon stands at each of the four corners of your
   tablecloth,
Drunk with your presence, sharing his meals with
   the poor.

Out of love for you, the unbeliever turns into a book
   of belief.
His soul is chosen. He becomes the king of true faith.

He is the jewel of the soul, the inspiration of speech,
The mountaintop that sees the road, the eyes that see
   the king.

Everyone drunk, who drank your wine, hands
   extended in prayer,
Praying to increase this love, finally says "Amen."

They say, "Recite sacred verses until your love is filled
   with peace."
For the soul weary of life, what is the use of reciting
   sacred verses?

Out of love, the lover kisses the ground.
In your kingdom, he tosses his saddle over the back
   of the sky.

Such happiness, the heart inseparable from the soul,
Sometimes reaching for the wine of the soul,
    sometimes the black hair.

The world never filled the saddlebags of my traveling
    soul.
My saddlebags were only filled by Shams, the truth
    of Tabriz.

Love, for the longest time, you have been my only friend

Love, for the longest time, you have been my
    only friend.
Tell me your secrets one by one. You are the eyes of
    the house.

Fearing your fire, I keep my mouth shut.
You are such a fire. You are such a flame.

You destroy the city of intellect with your breath.
You are the wind extinguishing intellect's lamp.

You are a good friend or a good enemy.
You go between them and you look like both.

Sages say, "The breath of a lover is a myth."
Why do I stay awake night and day if you are a myth?

You reveal your good will in adversity.
Your love is a test and you are its target.

King of kings, pride of Tabriz, Shams al-Din
Light of the earth and grandeur of the world!

Musician, strum the strings of the rabab of my heart

Musician, strum the strings of the rabab of my heart.
Listen to the sad lament as my heart responds to you.
Within every ruin, another treasure is hidden.
Love is the hidden treasure in the ruin of my heart.

My heart pulled me by my robe to the alley of my friend

My heart pulled me by my robe to the alley of
    my friend,
The alley where I drank wine and gave away my shoes
    and turban.

I lost my mind and grabbed his hair from behind.
Now within the curls of his hair, I'm trapped,
    I'm trapped.

Don't you see how I'm feeling as the wine keeps
    flowing?
Because of this rare, vintage wine, I've lost my mind.

He said, "When you are drunk, hide the secrets you
    have of mine."
Muslims, I ask you! When I am drunk, how can I hide
    my secrets?

The beloved says to me, "For a lover, annihilation is
    preferable."
My beloved, why are you in such a rush? Don't you see
    I'm busy?

Like a spring cloud, I'm crying and smiling at the
    same time.
From such strong wine, I'm both sober and drunk.

When you see the divine bird flying, from love, over
    Mount Qaf,
When the mountain hears from his beloved's ruby lips,
    I will run faster.

From love of Shams of Tabriz, I'm like two strings
    of heaven.
Draw the bow slowly so as not to break my rabab.

Lift up your head, my friend. Behold my pale face

Lift up your head, my friend. Behold my pale face.
I've made my life a shield but don't shoot too
    many arrows.

From all the arrows, my heart is like a porcupine's
    back.
If love had a heart, your love would have mercy on me.

I'm letting my heart go. Whatever it wants, so be it.
Slap your hand on my mouth if I ever speak of it again.

I'm the drunken slave of the wine bearer of love.
Sleeping in a corner, drunk, I'm free from good
    and evil.

If sorrow comes, I say, "The one who was in pain
    just left.
Get yourself to the bazaar and buy a rabab for me
    to play."

My heart longs for the cries of a clarion trumpet

My heart longs for the cries of a clarion trumpet.
With the clarion call comes the scent of the beloved.

With all my soul, I am longing for a love song,
In whose cries my beautiful beloved will appear.

I am weeping, as I am pregnant with sorrow.
How marvelous that this weeping soul should
    give birth.

Sing, flute, of the feelings of lovers,
For your song tests my soul.

Listen, soul, for the sound of the drum,
When even the new moon begins to shine.

Recite this chant from the page of the heart,
Until even the angels begin to weep.

When such cries comfort those in need,
Commands to be quiet will never silence them.

Looking for you, I return

Looking for you, I return.
Towards your sea, I return.

The waves of your sorrow swept away the house of
    my heart.
Quickly to your shore, I return.

My head is a pot boiling with longing for you.
Towards your head filled with longing, I return.

From your head, you toss a hundred ropes.
Climbing towards your highest height, I return.

The clarion moan of your trumpet reaches my soul.
Looking for your trumpet, I return.

Jump up! The soul of whirling is rising to its feet

Jump up! The soul of whirling is rising to its feet.
That sweet tambourine is now the companion of
    that flute.
The old longing has once again been set on fire.
Where are your shouts? Now is the time for shouting!

In harmony with your friend, you will never be alone

In harmony with your friend, you will never be alone.
In harmony with your customer, you will never
    be poor.
The moon keeps its light by not fearing the darkness.
In harmony with its thorns, the rose keeps its scent.

Everyone is dancing, and, again, the day begins

Everyone is dancing, and, again, the day begins.
Giving life to daylight, the day begins.

We whirled for a few nights and days,
In sadness and in joy until the day begins.

Many towns in the world are covered in night.
At this hour, in this place, the day begins.

Everyone is sleeping in the blind night.
When love's sunlight comes to me, the day begins.

Day never comes to those who are not lovers.
For lovers filled with passion, the day begins.

Don't look for morning in the corner of this house.
Turn your face on high, for on high, the day begins.

Though you grow thorns, roses blossom for me.
Though you are in night, for me, the day begins.

If you are a child, not yet aware of the day,
Get up with me, your loving father, the day begins.

Don't deny the day. Don't cry "No, no."
How long asleep? For your loving teacher, the
    day begins.

The sun rose, "the moon was split."
Listen to this exalted decree, as the day begins.

O Watchman, enough! Don't sound your alarm.
My watchman and my sentinel, the day begins.

Wake up, dance for joy. Press yourself against me

Wake up, dance for joy. Press yourself against me,
Flash your eyes, and make the evil eye blind.

Press yourself against me. Bring the dead to life.
Like Jesus, with true sorcery, raise the dead.

Your face more beautiful than the moon, bring it close
   to mine,
Until I see hundreds of eternal worlds.

I truly saw you. I tasted your sugar.
On the paper you gave me, I kissed your name.

You were my dear angel. What happened, God?
You were always telling us, "Who begets no son."

When I took your hand, I didn't see your face,
I fainted and I lost my mind.

Give me the cup of wine, like fire, with no mercy,
Until I lose myself, not knowing good or evil.

Fill my cup this time to the brim,
Until my eyes are filled and envy disappears.

Give me wine from above, where there is no God
   but God,
Until God sees and destroys the bodies of the dead.

From my body in its rough robe, all traces of reason
    gone,
Now, as much as you wish, press yourself against me.

Come, come, soul of the soul of the soul of whirling

Come, come, soul of the soul of the soul of whirling,
A thousand candles, illuminating the house of
    whirling.

The hearts of a hundred thousand stars lit by you.
Come, you are the full moon in the sky of whirling.

Come, the soul and the world mesmerized by
    your face.
Come, you marvelous creature in the world of
    whirling.

Come, without you no trading in love's bazaar.
Come, your gold never seen in the mine of whirling.

Come, those who long for you are sitting at the door.
Lower down from your rooftop the ladder of whirling.

Come, wealth to love's bazaar from your lips,
A great beauty hidden within the shop of whirling.

Bring the sugar of meaning from Shams of Tabriz,
Kept open by love are the lips of whirling.

Last night, without you, was dark and hopeless

Last night, without you, was dark and hopeless.
Our candles and whirling and gatherings had no flavor.

I was tortured all night, though I had committed
   no crime.
My heart was in prison with no one to pay the ransom.

The world feels safe in your embrace.
Even the moon, not seeing your face, grows anxious.

Our pride has become like a curtain covering you.
Only the humble are held in your embrace.

My modest heart is held in the palm of your hand,
Like quicksilver, quivering in your palm.

I'm your friend, I'm your friend, the friend of your sorrow

I'm your friend, I'm your friend, the friend of
    your sorrow.
When I came to your side, I left everyone else behind.

The sky said to me, "I'm tired of your whirling."
I said, "This center has turned me into a compass."

I hear such uproar day and night from the dome of
    the heart.
Like the dome of the heart, I became a whirling
    heavenly vault.

Suddenly falling, like a voice, into the harp of
    your sorrow,
Desiring your plucking, I turned one by one into
    its strings.

Sorrow hides its neck, avoiding the slaps of my hand.
In the forest of the soul, I turned into the lion of God.

When I saw his wine, I turned into a cheap
    drinking cup.
When I saw his hat, I lost my heart and I lost my head.

When the holy man of my heart gave me amazing
    wine,
Dancing, and trailing my robe, I passed through
    the tavern.

The master of freedom said to me, "Patience will free
you from sin."
Don't say another word. Because of this freedom,
I am trapped.

The sky kept whirling constantly until I began
to whirl.
My friend kept crying constantly until I entered
the cave.

At midnight in moonlight I began walking towards
the path.
Desiring his beauty, I made my way to the rose garden.

Like a lily, waiting to bloom, I became a poet and
storyteller.
Like a nightingale, singing until dawn, repeating
myself.

I became a tornado of thoughts. I became a hundred
different tasks.
When my heart beheld your work, I left my own work
behind.

How can my soul find peace, my friend?
With a touch!

How can my soul find peace, my friend? With a touch!
How can the sick recover from illness? With a touch!

No matter how many times you sit close to him,
    it's not enough.
Don't you see how he's sitting next to you right now?
    With a touch!

After ten days of thirst when will he be satisfied with
    a jug of water?
Only when the water has been sweetened.
    With a touch!

Seeking to be joined with you, he's not afraid of disgrace.
This year he wishes to dance again for joy.
    With a touch!

I'm working so hard, the world is laughing at me.
You fool, this task can be done simply. With a touch!

With just one touch a clay brick turns into a palace.
And a full garment turns into a single thread.
    With a touch!

In the midst of the field of your love, Shams, the truth
    of Tabriz,
A hundred gardens and roses turn into one thorn.
    With a touch!

Whirling brings peace to our souls

Whirling brings peace to our souls,
As you know, if your soul is alive.

If you're sleeping in a rose garden,
He wants you to wake up.

If you're asleep in a prison,
Then better to sleep forever.

Whirl at weddings,
Not at funerals, a place of crying.

If you don't know yourself,
And you don't see the moon,

What's the point of beating a drum?
Whirling brings together lovers of the heart.

If you're facing the *qibla*,
Whirl in this world and the next.

For the whirling circle,
The *Kaaba* is the center.

If you desire a field of sugar, it's there.
All fingers covered in sweetness are joined together.

I am a lover of love, not like every Muslim

I am a lover of love, not like every Muslim.
I am a tiny little ant, not like King Solomon.
All I have to offer is my pale face and torn heart,
Not like the butcher's shop in the bazaar.

At evening prayer, when the sun begins to set

At evening prayer, when the sun begins to set,
The doors of the senses shut, and the unseen
    is revealed.

The Angel of Sleep drives forth the spirits,
Like a shepherd tending his flocks.

Within the invisible spiritual meadows,
What cities and gardens he displays to them!

The soul sees a thousand marvelous faces and forms,
As sleep expunges all images of the world from him.

You might say, the soul always lived in that place,
And has forgotten this world and feels no yearning.

The body strains under the load of cares in this world.
The heart escapes without a trace of sadness.

You, who have gone on *hajj*. Where are you?

You, who have gone on *hajj*. Where are you? Where
    are you?
The beloved is here. Come here! Come here!

Your beloved is your neighbor and lives next door.
Are you lost in the desert and wandering?

When you see the faceless face of the beloved,
You are the master, the house, and the *Kaaba*.

Ten times you went on that road to that house.
One time, from this house, climb to the roof.

You described the beauty of that house of mercy,
Now describe for me the master of that house.

If you come from that garden, where is your bouquet
    of roses?
If you come from the sea of God, where is the pearl
    of your soul?

In the end, your suffering is your treasure.
How sad that you are the veil of your own treasure.

Congratulations! Here comes the month of fasting!

Congratulations! Here comes the month of fasting!
Have a good journey, dear friend of fasting.

I climbed to the roof to see the moon,
With all my heart and soul, I longed for fasting.

When I looked up, my hat fell off.
My head set spinning by the king of fasting.

Muslims, my head has been spinning since that day.
Such dignity, luck, and good fortune from fasting!

Inside this month is a hidden moon,
Hidden like a Turk in the tent of fasting.

You can find that hidden moon
In the joyous month of the harvest of fasting.

His satin face grows pale,
He wears the silken robe of fasting.

Prayers in this month are answered,
The skies torn apart by the sighs of fasting.

Like Joseph, beloved of the Pharaoh of Egypt,
Waiting patiently in the well of fasting.

Don't call for the dawn prayer. Be silent.
The faithful are awake if they are fasting.

Draw near, Shams al-Din, the Pride of Tabriz,
You are the commander for the army of fasting.

Today I saw your beauty, blessings upon you

Today I saw your beauty, blessings upon you.
A new desire twists about me, blessings upon you.

When roses bloom, they smile at the whole world.
Oh you, smiling at one rose, and a hundred roses,
    blessings upon you.

When angels see your face, they stumble and fall.
The heart at the door of this house, trembling,
    blessings upon you.

When I saw your face at Nowruz, I joyfully rained
    down tears,
Such a rain and such a Nowruz, blessings upon you.

Your lips speechless, your language without words,
Your ears listening to the within, blessings upon you.

That angelic face is the zenith of both worlds

That angelic face is the zenith of both worlds.
When he lifts his veil, Venus fades into nothingness.

When he rides the winged Buraq of sublime truth,
Who will be brave enough to join his kingdom?

The stars in the sky all go dark,
When this king tosses his dice on the board of heaven.

The Angel Gabriel sees him and bows to the ground.
The angels closest to God receive blessings from him.

Heavenly phoenix, the lord Shams of Tabriz,
The seven seas are like a drop before him.

Don't let your heart turn, the heart of your beloved knows

Don't let your heart turn, the heart of your beloved
    knows.
Don't hide your secrets, any of your secrets, he knows.

He brushes aside everything around you, like twigs
    on water,
Even the tricks of wine that only the drunken heart
    knows.

He plants thorns in his palm. Roses bloom in his palm.
All the roses hidden in the thorns of the heart
    he knows.

Every day, little by little, you learn another lesson.
Go, be his apprentice, as everything all at once
    he knows.

A prisoner at the time of judgment, you witness
    and confess,
The confession of the heart, the body of the Sufi
    already knows.

Last night I dreamed I was poor

Last night I dreamed I was poor,
Nearly fainting from such grace.

Astonished and delirious until dawn,
By the beauty and perfection of poverty.

I saw this poverty as a mine of rubies,
Its hues clothing me like a red silk robe.

I heard the din and clamor of lovers.
I heard the sounds of their cups clinking.

I saw them in a ring, drunk with poverty,
And wore a slave's ring in my ear.

I saw many visions in the light of poverty.
I saw many visions of life on its face.

Within my soul a hundred waves arose,
As I saw the ocean begin to churn.

The sky thundered a hundred thousand cries:
O Slave, you are the leader of my caravan!

I was a trusted friend of the pilgrims on the road

I was a trusted friend of the pilgrims on the road.
I was a close companion of the people of Jerusalem.

I saw a dome that transcended the six earthly
  directions.
I turned into dirt and became a carpet beneath that
  dome.

I turned into blood, boiling in the veins of love,
I turned into wet tears in the eyes of love.

Sometimes like Jesus, I turned into words,
Sometimes like Mary, I turned into a silent heart.

Whatever you could not find in Jesus or Mary,
If you believed in me, I turned into that as well.

When everlasting love wounded me with its spear,
At a hundred spots, I turned into wounds and
  was cured.

I took each step with the Angel Azrael.
If I was separated from him, I lost my way.

Face to face with death, I went into battle.
I was brought to life by the eyes of death.

I was released from the heavy load of the world,
And fastened myself into the saddle of eternity.

Listen to me play the eternal flute,
Though I am bent like the back of a harp.

God the All-Knowing turned his face towards me.
Sacrificing my life for God, I became All-Knowing.

The greatest festival was Shams of Tabriz.
For this festival, I sacrificed my life.

The scent of the musk of Khotan comes to me

The scent of the musk of Khotan comes to me.
The scent of my shining friend comes to me.

The song of the nightingales sounds in my ear.
The scent of gardens and jasmine comes to me.

Like a pregnant woman, I endure labor pains.
In the meadow, the soul's infant comes to me.

The perfumed hair of the pure soul,
Like a soul entering the body, comes to me.

My Joseph fell into the well of separation.
From the Pharaoh of Egypt, his robe comes to me.

I am the martyr of love. My shroud is bloody.
The blood money wrapped in my shroud comes to me.

I do not need to wear that crown on my head,
When in such a way his sweet chin comes to me.

I put my head like a candle on a plate.
Look as his head on a plate comes to me.

The souls stand row upon row on the rooftop of
    the body.
The king who disbands these rows comes to me.

As if the harp of delight has already been tuned,
So the song of bodies touching comes to me.

As if the wine bearer of the soul has been busy,
Such a wine poured in my mouth comes to me.

Or from the light of the agate ring of Mohammad,
The scent of the All-Merciful from Yemen comes
    to me.

Or from the scent of Shams of Tabriz,
Out of love, the roars of ecstasy come to me.

Simorgh takes flight from Mount Qaf again

Simorgh takes flight from Mount Qaf again.
The bird of my heart takes flight from my chest again.

The bird drunkenly searching for seeds,
Throws seeds in the fire, his heart beating again.

His sunken eyes bleed in the night of separation.
His eyes see the face of the morning again.

Mohammad and his companion together in the cave,
The spider weaves its web over the opening again.

The teeth of delight, set on edge, taste sour separation.
Today the sugar cane of unity is bit into again.

The black shirt, worn on the day of farewell,
Is ripped down to the navel again.

The noblewomen of Egypt looking at Joseph,
Slice the citrus fruits and their hands again.

Weeping Joseph seeks Zolaykha in the bazaar,
Trying to buy her with a jar of rubies again.

The fiery eyes of the deer belonging to the lion Joseph,
Graze among the fire of lovers again.

The matron's soul leaves the body's house.
Because of love, wearing her chador, she runs again.

In the pot, visions of the sweetheart not yet cooked,
On the three-legged stove, the visions cook again.

Look at Abraham at last among the milk and honey,
Licking the milk and honey off his fingers again.

The heart vowing never to sin, hiding from love,
Hears the magic spells of his beloved again.

On the rooftop of thought, my heart, in love, lying on
    his back,
Is counting the stars, one by one, again.

The passion of love, a gypsy stealing, covered in
    darkness,
Climbs up my hair like a rope to the rooftop again.

The moneychanger seeking the coin of love's essence,
Bites to test that coin in his palm.

The glory of Tabriz, Shams the truth,
Is pulling me by my ears towards himself again.

**I'm in love and crazed and driven mad
by Damascus**

I'm in love and crazed and driven mad by Damascus.
I gave my soul, heartsick for the passion of Damascus.

When, from that direction, the blessed morning shines,
Each dawn and dusk I'm drunk with the magic
    of Damascus.

At the Barid Gate, separated from the beloved,
Far from the congregation of lovers, in the paradise
    of Damascus.

Have you not drunk from the fountain of Bu Nuwas?
I'm in love with the arm of the water bearer
    of Damascus.

Let me swear an oath on Osman's holy book,
The pearl of that beloved, gleaming in Damascus.

Far from the Gate of Joy and the Gate of Paradise,
Who knows what visions I'm seeking in Damascus?

Let's climb to Rebva as if we're in the cradle of Christ,
Like monks, we're drunk on the red wine of Damascus.

In royal Nayrab, I saw a tree.
I sat in its shade and longed for Damascus.

Through green playing fields, like a ball, rolled
By a curl of hair, like a polo stick, towards Damascus.

When I arrive at Mezza Gate, I won't lack for tasty
    spice,
At the Eastern Gate, passing on to the heart
    of Damascus.

On the mount of Salehiye is a mine of pearls.
I dive for that pearl into the sea of Damascus.

Upon seeing Damascus, the paradise of the world,
I await a vision of the beautiful face of Damascus.

For the third time I gallop from Rome to Syria.
From dark Syrian curls, I catch the scent of Damascus.

If there I might be of service to Shams, the truth
    of Tabriz,
A servant in Damascus, I'll be the master of Damascus!

Sometimes you rip my veil, sometimes you sew

Sometimes you rip my veil, sometimes you sew.
Sometimes you build me up, sometimes you burn.
You taught me to be young when I was old.
Creator of the world, teach me to welcome old age.

On the path of unity, worship or sin

On the path of unity, worship or sin,
In the alley of the tavern, dervish or king,
The face of a holy man, bright or dark,
Above the dome of the heavens, sun or moon.

The scent of God comes from every direction

The scent of God comes from every direction.
Behold the crowds out of their minds with joy.

All souls are thirsty for the water he brings
As the thirsty hear the cries of the water bearer.

Babies wanting milk are worried and upset,
Wondering when their mothers will appear.

All are living in exile and separation,
Wondering when unity and communion will begin.

Every dawn you hear the sounds of prayer,
From Muslims, Christians, and Jews alike.

Blessed is he who hears with the ear of the heart,
The cries of the call to prayer falling from the skies.

Clean out the sounds of enmity from your ears,
To hear those cries falling from the heavens.

An impure ear cannot drink in those cries.
Every evil deed gets its due reward.

Don't cloud your eyes looking for dust and motes.
The Everlasting King is manifest before you.

If your eyes are cloudy, wash them with your tears,
For in those tears, you will discover the remedy.

The sugar caravan has arrived from Egypt.
The sounds of clapping and bells can now be heard.

Be silent for the rest of this ghazal,
The King of All Speech is among us.

Your glow through the window is our summer

Your glow through the window is our summer.
Like warm-heated summer, lead us to our rose garden.

Medicine for the eyes of the soul, where have you gone!
    Come back!
So the water of mercy will flow in the midst of our
    circle of fire.

Deserts will turn green. Graves will turn to gardens.
Sour grapes will turn sweet. Freshly baked will be our
    bread.

Sunlight of the heart and soul, the sun pales before you.
Do you see how mud and water has caked our souls?

Out of love for your face, thorns turned to rose
    gardens.
A hundred thousand vows were planted within our
    faith.

Face of eternal love, you turn your face gently towards
    the dead.
From out of our prisons, take our souls to The One.

From the smoke of sorrow make joy. From the heart
    of night make day,
A day strange and wondrous, you, our radiant
    morning!

You turn glass beads to jewels. You open the heart
   of Venus.
You turn paupers to kings. Praise to you, our king.

Where are the eyes that can see you? So they can
   draw near.
Where is your ear that can hear? So you can listen
   to our logic.

The heart is measuring your mercy, grateful for that
   sugar cane.
Its flavor and taste cry out from the roots of our teeth.

From our souls come the sound of drums, until the
   parts became whole,
Basil to sweet basil, rose to rose, freed from the prison
   of our thorns.

I cry so many cries, my face so pale

I cry so many cries, my face so pale,
Until I wipe the rust from the mirror of doubt.

The heart rides in the saddle of your love,
At every step traveling miles towards the soul.

Show your bright ruby in the blind darkness,
Until stones from the sky rain on the heads of the
    stone-hearted.

In your radiance, why do they deny you?
In your kingdom and glory, they are a shame and
    a disgrace.

If they are blind, in the end, they will finally see,
Faraway, thousands of souls hanging from the moon
    like stars.

From the joy of your light, the blind will see,
From the joy of your path, the crippled will walk.

Sometimes the mind gets lost on your path.
Since poppies grow in your green fields.

On your path, I see many lamenting like empty-hearted
    flutes.
On your path, two hundred swaying cypresses bend
    from sorrow, like harps.

On your path, thousands of caravans were broken
    down.
On your path, many capsized ships were sunk in
    the Ganges.

The souls of the broken put their hopes in you,
Until they find wisdom in your endless knowledge,

Until you lift oppression with your kindness upon
    kindness,
Until all sides find peace, until wars fade away,

Until we seek another way, walk along another way,
Taking heart in the harmony of linking arm in arm,

Shams of Tabriz accepts that joyful invitation,
With every atom of desire, every hair on his noble
    head.

Once again my cunning lover found me

Once again my cunning lover found me.
In the bazaar, he drunkenly found me.

Hiding from his languorous gaze,
I escaped from the tavern where he found me.

Why bother? No one can hide from him.
Why hide? A hundred times, he found me.

I said, "Who can find me in a crowded city?"
In the crowd of my secrets, he found me.

Good news! Those amorous eyes glanced at me.
How lucky! Deft and curly-haired, he found me.

He stole turbans from drunken heads.
Hiding in the folds of my turban, he found me.

While I pulled a thorn from the sole of my foot,
That cypress of two hundred flowerbeds found me.

He scattered roses on my head from his garden.
That rare nightingale once again found me.

I was lost in the halo of the full moon.
Today, in the cellar, that moon found me.

On the path, dropped a trace of my blood.
Following the trail of blood, he found me.

Like a deer, I ran from the lion towards the desert.
That lion, in hunting season, in the mountains,
    found me.

Able to leap as high as the sky to capture a deer,
Patiently and deliberately, in a crossing, he found me.

At the bottom of the sea, his fishhook caught in
    my mouth.
Caught by his deadly hook, the hunter found me.

Giving me a cup of wine to relieve my heartache,
At that moment, my gentle beloved found me.

My heavy soul lightly rose up and flew away,
That precious jeweled cup, light headed, found me.

Today I don't need mind or ear or tongue.
The source of all thought and speech has found me.

What tent did you pitch above the world of eternity?

What tent did you pitch above the world of eternity,
When you created the world within your mind?

Why did you curl the hair of impiety about the face
    of faith,
Intent on Muslims, and Christians, and Infidels alike?

Wave upon wave of your glorious light shone through
    the soul.
In the sea of the soul, you held together the sea and
    the pearl.

In the presence of your astonishing love, all lions
    became pupils.
They trembled and fell down as you helped them
    up again.

You captured souls, sometimes poor, sometimes
    imprisoned,
And sometimes you made them sultans, and kings,
    and princes.

You burned a hundred thousand in the sea,
And kept a hundred thousand damp in the fire.

Inside one human body, a talisman,
Holds the sun and moon and the wheel of the sky
    and stars.

In such a body, like a coffin in blood and dirt,
You brought endless joy to this martyr, the soul.

O sunrise, before you, each atom gave thanks
and bowed,
As you poured sugar into their mouths, full
of gratitude.

You sprinkled the salt of your life onto this mortal life,
Making it as fresh and fragrant as musk and
ambergris.

Shams of Tabriz, out of your love I am hammering
gold,
Since you filled the highs and lows of love with gold.

Without you, I am banished from my life

Without you, I am banished from my life.
Without you, I would never choose my life.

Without your joyful face, being alive
Is like a death in the name of life.

You are the world's cure and its poison.
You are the seed and the bird trap of life.

You are a jewel and this world a jewel box.
You are both the wine and the goblet of life.

Without your water, the rose garden is a desert.
Without your boiling, all that is left is raw life.

Without your fine and upright stature,
Justice is nowhere to be found in life.

I have many wishes and desires, but without you,
I can never satisfy any of my wishes in life.

Since you have not been calling aloud "Salaam,"
Who will ever be able to call aloud "Salaam" to life?

I remain silent. Like a king, rule your kingdom,
And your servant will always and forever be life.

The day my soul travels to the heavens

The day my soul travels to the heavens,
And the parts of my body scatter like dust,
With your finger, write in my dust, "Rise up!"
I'll spring from my tomb as my body pulls back
    my soul.

If I die, carry me away

If I die, carry me away,
And bring my dead body to my beloved.
If he kisses my pale lips,
Don't be amazed if I come back to life.

When I die and my coffin is carried out

When I die and my coffin is carried out,
Don't think I'm in pain, leaving this world.

Don't weep for me, don't sigh and mourn.
Only if the devil pulls you down, sigh and mourn.

When you see my corpse, don't cry, "He's gone!"
I long for that time and for that reunion.

When you bury me, don't cry, "Farewell!"
The grave is but the shroud of paradise.

When you see the setting, wait for the rising.
What is the harm in a sunset or a fading moon?

You think it is setting but it is rising.
When the tomb imprisons, the soul is set free.

What seed dropped into the ground did not grow?
Why doubt the seed of your own humanity?

What bucket dropped into a well comes up empty?
Why would a soul in Jacob's well shout for help?

When you close your mouth here, open it there.
Your cries and shouts will fill the sky beyond the sky.

If wheat grows from my soil

If wheat grows from my soil,
The bread you bake will make you drunk.

Both dough and baker are crazy.
The oven recites a drunken poem.

If you visit my grave,
My tomb will make you dance.

Be sure to bring a tambourine.
Don't be sad at God's festival.

My chin is shut, within the grave, asleep,
My mouth gnawing on bittersweet love.

If you rip apart my shroud,
A drunken man will unravel your soul.

From all sides, sounds of war and drunken harps,
Empty tasks become fruitful works.

God created me from love's wine.
I'm still that love even as death wears me down.

I'm the drunken man. My essence is the wine of love.
What do you expect from wine but drunkenness?

I will never rest until my soul flies
To the towering soul of Shams of Tabriz.

What will I do if death comes to take me away?

What will I do if death comes to take me away?
I'll sprinkle a hundred souls on him and welcome him
    joyfully.

I'll go to heaven dancing, pulled towards eternity.
You've taken away my patience. Please come sooner!

You take away the stars from the moon, piece by piece.
Sometimes you take the baby, sometimes the nurse.

My heart is an entire world, bearing a great mountain.
Since I can bear a mountain, why should I carry straw?

When my hair turns white as milk, I grow old out of
    joy for death.
I am flour, not wheat. Why did I ever come to this mill?

In the mill, the grain is the child of a stalk of wheat.
I'm the child of the moon, not the stalk. Why am I still
    here?

No moonlight falls through the cracks in the mill.
It returns to the moon, never passing through
    the bakery.

When I'm in touch with my wisdom, I have worthy
    things to say.
Be silent, so the morning breeze doesn't overhear
    our speech.

When you died, your eyes gazed into the world of the spirit

When you died, your eyes gazed into the world of
   the spirit.
When you were born again, all at once you knew
   how to live.

Whoever died and returned to life, raised up
   like Enoch,
Became an angelic teacher with knowledge of
   the unknown.

By what road did you travel from this world?
And by what secret road did you return?

The road where souls fly each night,
Each night the cages of city upon city are emptied of
   their birds.

If the bird's talons are tied, he cannot fly.
He will never reach the circle of heaven. He is an exile.

In dying, he cuts his attachments and flies away,
Able to see the truth and mystery of all things.

Be silent. The world of silence is like a bird's wing.
Don't beat the drum of words. That drum is sadly
   empty.

In the book of my life only one page remains

In the book of my life only one page remains.
His sweet jealousy has left my soul dismayed.

In my book, he wrote words sweeter than sugar,
Words that would make the shy moon blush.

Eternity illuminates the page of the rose garden.
No fears of change or passing time remain.

His name fills my final page, his everlasting kingdom,
Where the secrets of the saints are written in twilight.

The light of God wraps around him like a page,
Shams, the truth of Tabriz, the light within our eyes.

In the clean, pure sea, I dissolved like salt

In the clean, pure sea, I dissolved like salt,
No faith, no lack of faith, no certainty, no doubt.
I found a star inside my heart.
The seven heavens disappeared within that star.

From a lovely thought, my spirit comes alive

From a lovely thought, my spirit comes alive,
Inviting the bride of poetry into my wedding chamber.
In every verse, a thousand young women appear,
All of them, like Mary, pregnant and virgin.

Open your eyes and look. From the body, souls are escaping

Open your eyes and look. From the body, souls
    are escaping
The soul has broken its cage. From the body, the heart
    is escaping.

Look at the hundred thousand intellects that have
    vanished.
A hundred thousand selves are selflessly escaping.

If a hundred thousand hearts and souls escape,
    I'm happy.
When they arrive drunk and smiling, from me they
    are escaping.

A hundred thousand souls looking for water left
    the body,
A hundred thousand nightingales to the meadows
    escaping.

From my heart arose the army of the soul

From my heart arose the army of the soul.
An army both seen and unseen, they arose.

Tearing apart my garments of patience,
On the path of the soul, garments torn, they arose.

The brides of the soul tore off their veils.
Seeing the king of the world, they arose.

Like a stream, they flowed from on high.
Dancing towards the earth, they arose.

The face of the heart shattered all other faces.
The gatekeepers seeking a kingdom, they arose.

Whatever was seen, unseen they arose.
Whatever was unseen, seen they arose.

Whoever was renowned, their name vanished.
Whoever was unknown, with a name they arose.

A moon appeared in the dawn sky

A moon appeared in the dawn sky.
Coming down from the sky, he looked at me.

Like a hawk that seized a little bird while hunting,
That moon seized me and climbed back into the sky.

I looked into myself but there was no self there.
Within that tender moon, my body became a soul.

I traveled within my soul and saw nothing but
    the moon,
Until the primordial secret was revealed and explained.

Nine heavenly spheres were immersed within
    that moon.
The entire ship of my existence vanished in that sea.

The sea surged until reason rose again,
And a voice was heard talking about this and that.

The sea foamed and out of that sparkling foam
An image appeared and a body appeared.

All the foam of the body received a sign from the sea.
All at once the foam melted and floated into the sea.

Without the good fortune of Shams, the truth
    of Tabriz,
No one can see the moon or be transformed into
    the sea.

**Look into the face of the beloved until his hues
come alive**

Look into the face of the beloved until his hues
    come alive.
As the hues reflect in your face, O pale one, come alive!

Every atom is whirling until they feel alive.
You, atom, don't you wish to come alive?

You were like a stone. Touched by his life,
Sweet running streams from stones come alive.

In the mirror, I looked into a vision of transcendence.
I asked, "Who are you?" He said, "I am light
    come alive."

In the life everlasting, you will find everyone alive.
Who are those left behind? Longing to come alive?

The truly alive are at peace, having seized their lives.
The cowardly are left behind, battling to come alive.

Sir, don't you see this Judgment Day?

Sir, don't you see this Judgment Day?
Don't you see this Joseph of goodness, tall and strong?

Master, don't you see this pearl of wisdom?
This radiant light, this dignity and glory?

Lord, don't you see this kingdom of the soul?
This royal garden, this blessing and fortune?

My pious and respectable friend, are you crazy or am I?
Drink wine with me. Let go of finding fault.

Revolving moon, you always stay full,
Your magnificent light erases all sins.

When you see running water, leave ritual behind.
At the Festival of Unity, leave austerity behind.

If you flirt, you are young. If you respond, mature.
Taking on suffering, you find sweetness and beauty.

Be silent! Silence is better than tasting honey.
Burn away logic. Leave behind wordplay.

Shams of Tabriz, your east gives life.
From your glow, the sun grows warm.

Each day, full of joy, seek a new place to live

Each day, full of joy, seek a new place to live,
Like running water, free from dirt and stones.
Winter is past, like yesterday, and so is winter's tale.
Today we must find a new tale to tell.

You're at peace when you don't need more or less

You're at peace when you don't need more or less,
When you don't need to be a king or a saint,
When you're free from the sorrows of the world,
When you're free from the tiniest atom of yourself.

Finally, you broke away and made your way to the unseen

Finally, you broke away and made your way to
　　the unseen.
How amazing! By what road did you leave this world?

You spread your feathered wings and smashed
　　your cage.
You took flight and traveled to the world of souls.

You were a royal falcon caught by an old woman.
When you heard the distant drums, you flew into
　　the beyond.

You were a drunken nightingale among the owls.
You caught the scent of the garden and flew to gather
　　roses.

You were intoxicated with sour wine,
Until you flew to the everlasting tavern.

You were like an arrow, aimed at the target of bliss.
Released from the bow, you flew towards the target.

This ghoulish world gave you false clues.
You left behind all clues and flew into the sublime.

Why do you need a crown when you are the sun?
Why look for a mountain when you have left
　　this world?

I've heard two dead eyes will look for the soul.
Why look for the soul when you have flown to the soul
of souls?

Heart, you are a rare bird, hunting after the hunter.
Using your two wings as a shield, you flew towards the
point of the arrow:

Fleeing autumn, the amazing rose was joyful.
Walking through autumn breezes, slowly, slowly
you went.

Like rain from the sky, you fell on the world's rooftops.
Wherever you went, water flowed from the rainwater
pipes.

Be silent! Cut short all this talk, and go to sleep!
You have found refuge with your beloved friend.

Caged bird, don't fly with the bird of paradise!

Caged bird, don't fly with the bird of paradise!
You don't have wings. Don't long for the desert.

Don't crawl like a salamander into the heart of fire.
If you go, you will only disgrace yourself.

O Tailor, blacksmithing is not for you.
If you don't know how, don't try to start a fire.

First, learn the art from blacksmiths.
If you haven't taken a lesson, don't begin.

Since you're not an ocean, don't go to the ocean.
Don't long for the waves and majesty of the sea.

If you do, hold tight to the stern of the ship.
Don't loosen your grip on the ship's edge.

If you must fall, fall back into the ship,
Don't rely on your fingers and your toes.

If you long to go to heaven, speak of Jesus,
Otherwise don't set out for heaven's dome.

You're a raw fruit. Cling to the branch.
Don't leave the treetop without maturity.

Shams of Tabriz dwells with the Most High,
Not wishing to be perched anywhere but there.

This happy morning kissed me three times

This happy morning kissed me three times.
This happy morning blessed me.

My heart, remember your dream last night,
Before happy morning opened its door for me.

In your dream, I saw the moon pick me up,
Take me to the sky, and leave me.

I saw my heart, humble and broken at love's feet.
At this moment I began singing a song that came to me.

Between love and my heart, much was going on,
Little by little, the memory comes back to me.

It might seem as if I gave birth to love,
But no, truly, love gave birth to me.

Your hidden qualities are visible, your very essence.
I swear by your essence, you are all desire to me.

I feel but don't see the kiss you sent me.
Through the layers of nature, I don't know who sent it
    to me.

Have mercy on me as I fall into oblivion.
I shouted from the beyond, "Who will help me?"

Although I was cursed instead of kissed,
Luckily that curse has brought wisdom to me.

Fortune made me smile, at last

Fortune made me smile, at last.
Pulled the horse's bridle this way, at last.

The wings of the bird of the heart were closed.
Fortune gave the bird wings to fly, at last.

Knowledge made the garden smile,
And the cloud was crying, at last.

Such a great victory greeted me
Such a great land was seized, at last.

Struck by a loyal polo stick, the golden ball
Rolled through this field, at last.

Mars undid his belt and threw it away.
Swords were clanging together, at last.

The sky is smiling at the earth,
Since God has freed the earth from fear, at last.

God gave me wine and gave you vinegar

God gave me wine and gave you vinegar.
Since fate brought us together, why fight?

Wine is a rose and its thorns a hangover.
He knows all things and judges them fairly.

Your desire will never turn sweet into sour,
The heart of sweet pastry is filled with sugar.

He gave you the job of a mourner, so mourn.
He made me his musician, so I play the horn.

Sweet, sweet, when my lover smiles at me.
When I look at his face, I am set free from lies.

If your sugar turns sour because of me,
Accept the sour. Don't let your anger grow.

If a rose cries in the world, I cry, too,
And mourn, like the roses.

My pain only let me search for rhymes.
Then he set me free, even from poetry.

Rip this poem apart like an old piece of cloth,
To set meaning free from words, wind, and air.

Whatever you hide from this king, he knows

Whatever you hide from this king, he knows.
If you cry without mouth or tongue, he knows.
Everyone wishes to sell his words.
I am the servant of the one who knows silence.

Because of you, I burn with sorrow, O God

Because of you, I burn with sorrow, O God.
All night long, the sky has been weeping.

The sky weeps and smiles,
Out of desire for the earth.

From so many tears pouring on the earth,
The earth was perfumed with tears.

From the weeping of the sky,
A hundred smiling rose gardens grew.

Last night I wept along with the sky.
The sky and I share a single faith.

What grew from the weeping of the sky?
Dewy green flowers and violets.

What grew from the weeping of the lovers?
A hundred delights from a pair of sweet lips.

The eyes feel the pressure of the tears.
The throat of the beloved grows tight.

The weeping cloud, the smiling earth,
Were joined together by you and me.

Our weeping and our smiling
Together made all things harmonious.

Be silent and observe.
Be a seeker of the purpose of the world.

I am a madman and I give birth to madmen

I am a madman and I give birth to madmen.
Look at me. I am shouting mad shouts.

Don't run from me. If you fall into my trap,
Say: "Thank God, I have fallen into his trap."

Love is strange and I am even stranger,
As if I created love out of myself.

Come here, even if you shed my blood.
Unless I die, I will never be born again.

I promise not to whisper your secret in words.
Only by not speaking is the secret untied.

Don't think! Don't think!

Don't think! Don't think! Thinking,
Like fire, burns everything fresh down to the root.

Be foolish! Be foolish! Drunk and bewildered,
Until all the fields of cane turn to sugar.

Don't think! Courage is crazy. Step into it.
Like lions and men, put vanity behind you.

Thinking is a trap, preventing sacrifice.
Why hide the truth for a spoonful of food?

When I shut my mouth, I am free of deceit.
When hunger cries out, I pretend I am deaf.

Yesterday I went to him full of dismay

Yesterday I went to him full of dismay.
He sat silently, not asking what was wrong.

I looked at him, waiting for him to ask,
"How were you yesterday without my luminous face?"

My friend instead was looking at the ground.
Meaning to say, Be like the ground, humble
   and wordless.

I bowed and kissed the ground.
Meaning to say, I am like the ground, drunk
   and amazed.

Traveling from this world, you went away

Traveling from this world, you went away.
From all its misery and trials, you went away.

O vision, you went towards your creator,
Into the soul of souls, you went away.

Taking sustenance from the tree of faith,
From this cruel home, you went away.

Swimming in the water of life like a fish,
Traveling far from this dust, you went away.

Passing through astrological houses like the sun,
Beyond the stars of the sky, you went away.

You rejoiced in the mine to which you returned,
From this house and this shop, you went away.

Revealing the road you followed,
In truth, by the hidden road, you went away.

Walking in a sacred circle on the world's roof,
Like water through a rain pipe, you went away.

Silence! Now, in the silence,
Away from all the silence, you went away.

Sometimes, in my childhood, I was a teacher

Sometimes, in my childhood, I was a teacher.
Sometimes I made my friends happy.
Listen to my story to hear what happened next.
I came like a cloud and I went like the wind.

Acknowledgments

I wish to acknowledge William Paterson University for granting release time from teaching for pursuing this project. We also wish to thank for their help and inspiration: Salar Abdoh; Qhasem Hasheminejad; Joy Harris; Barbara Heizer; Daniel Rafinejad; Paul Raushenbush; and Diana Secker Tesdell.

INDEX

The numbers for the ghazals and robaiyat (a hash sign followed by a number) follow the numbering in Foruzanfar's edition of *Kolliyat-e Shams ya Divan-e Kabir*, 10 vols (Tehran: University of Tehran Press, 1957-67), which was subsequently reprinted in a complete edition by Amir Kabir Press (Tehran: Amir Kabir Press, 1977).